CRUSH YOUR INSECURITIES

A RADICAL WAY TO APPROACH MODERN-AGED
INSECURITIES, UNDERSTAND THEM AND ELEVATE
OUR SELF-CONFIDENCE

J.C. RAGNERS

THE ULTIMATE SELF CARE ACTION PLAN

1. With this plan, you can instantly transform a bad day into a good one.
2. Scientifically proven by the experts.
3. Easy to adapt and implement without much effort.

To receive your confidence hack cheat sheet, visit the link-

http://www.jcragners.com/

CONTENTS

INTRODUCTION

Do you ever wish you could tell your insecurities to just fuck off? So you could feel all your worries, all your fears, all your doubts disappear? Instead, you'd be left with the peace of mind you've always wanted. You could enter any room, filled with any number of people of any age, gender, or background. And you could approach them with genuine self-confidence. The kind of confidence that establishes you as the type of person other people love to be around.

Or maybe you keep waiting for that quiet moment by yourself when suddenly it hits you. For the first time, you realize that you're truly happy. You know that there's nothing you would change about yourself, even if you had the opportunity. That you love yourself just as much as you love your partner, your friends, and your family members. That you deserve love just as much as your beautiful partner, your talented best friend, your crazy smart sibling, or even your loyal pet dog.

Whatever your circumstances are, you're hoping for a miracle. A quick fix to a lifelong problem that you have no clue how to solve on your own. Even as it tears you apart. Bit by bit. Every single day.

I feel your pain. When you struggle with insecurity, it's natural to hope for pessimism, all that anxiety, obsessing over the past or the future to go away with a snap of your fingers. Just like that! Never to return again. Unfortunately, this magic moment doesn't exist in real life. Insecurities are a pain in the ass that way. No one is entirely immune to them.

"At times, even the most self-assured people we know can feel like they're drowning in their insecurities. What sets them apart from less confident people is their mindset for success (Espinosa, 2017)."

Even the most confident people have days where they don't feel their best. Most of the time, we don't notice when they do. This is because confident people don't run away from their negative thoughts and beliefs. Instead, they confront them with courage. They assert their self-worth, embrace their imperfections, and refuse to let a bad experience ruin their day. Instead of crumbling under the pressures of insecurity, they emerge the better for it, seeing their hardships as opportunities for personal growth. Those tiny insecurities can't help but give way to the mighty power of self-assurance.

This incredible confidence may seem out of reach. But with the right mindset, anyone can overcome their insecurities, no matter how big they are or how many there are. All you need to know is where they come from, how they affect you, and how you can tell them to get lost whenever they start to mess with your head.

This book will help you understand what insecurity is and why it happens. It will introduce you to some common insecure behaviors like jealousy, comparison, unworthiness, validation, self-sabotage, social anxiety, bragging, overthinking, and defense mechanisms. It will outline the symptoms and root causes of each type of insecurity. It will also provide expert-recommended solutions, so you can take all your negative beliefs, thoughts, and actions, and throw them in the trash where they belong. The result? You'll be left with a new appreciation for all the weird and wonderful things that make you who you are.

"With a solid understanding of your insecurities and the right tools to overcome them, you can pull yourself out of the depths of despair and into the happy, confident life that you deserve (Buscher, 2018)."

As an immigrant kid, I'm no stranger to insecurity. I moved to Canada when I was young and faced a lot of difficulties during my school days. I always felt like a nerd who never really fit in. Too afraid to talk to anyone, I would look for new ways to escape uncomfortable social situations. As a teenager, parties were a constant struggle for me. Not only because I was shy, but also because everyone around me seemed so perfect, confident, and beautiful—unlike me. There were so many times when all I wanted to do was just disappear!

At the same time, however, I was curious about human behavior. Even when I was desperately trying to avoid people, I was still interested in learning why they act the way they do. I wanted to learn what motivates them and what makes them feel certain emotions. I was fascinated by how humans have this endless supply of creative solutions to solve complicated problems throughout their everyday lives.

Eventually, I realized that running away wasn't a very creative or effective solution to my complicated life problem. Instead, I had to find a way to overcome my insecurities. Facing my fears and learning from them was my first step toward gaining the confidence I always wanted.

My newfound self-assurance inspired me to study human psychology and behavior, which I've been doing for a decade now. I focus on insecurities, the root causes behind them, and the paradigm shift that changes the way we look at these insecurities. We should no longer see our so-called negative qualities as shameful aspects of ourselves that we have to hide away and imagine out of existence. Instead, we should work to become more courageous, so we can embrace our insecurities and use them to our full advantage.

There are so many things I know now that I wish I knew when I was younger. If I did, I could have been that cool, confident guy at parties that everyone loves to be around. And I wouldn't have had to change any of my dominant personality traits. I only would have had to change how I viewed myself and how I presented that view to others.

Now I'm making up for the lost time. And once you've finished this book, you can do the same. I hope that you'll find this information as useful as I did, so you can finally say goodbye to your insecurities and hello to the happy, self-assured life that you deserve.

Who knows? One day you could be helping others overcome their own negative self-perceptions.

Until then, you'll need a solid understanding of the different types of insecurities and their strategies to overcome them. Let's get started by taking a closer look at what insecurity is and why it happens to good people.

1

INSECURITY – WHAT IT IS, WHY WE HAVE IT

Insecurity is one of those abstract concepts that we tend to take for granted. It shapes so much of our daily life, including how we perceive ourselves and how we interact with others. Yet, we hardly ever stop to think about what it means, where it comes from, and why it makes our lives a living hell.

Once you know what insecurity is and why we experience it, you'll be able to pinpoint the root causes of your own insecurities, whether it's continuously obsessing over past decisions, worrying about future outcomes, or never feeling like you're smart/good-looking/talented enough to accomplish anything right now. Enlightened by this knowledge, you'll be ready to face your fears, worries, and doubts. You'll finally be able to tell them to get the fuck out of your life and leave you in peace.

WHAT IS INSECURITY?

Unlike other animals, humans are gifted with the blessing and the curse of self-consciousness (Collinson, 2003; Watts, 2011). Especially in the West, we like to separate ourselves from nature and society and position ourselves as unique individuals. We compare and contrast ourselves with other individuals, recognizing that their beliefs, opinions, and habits are different from ours. We can also reflect on the things we've done in the past. Realize that the present is impermanent. Change our actions to create a different version of the future. In short, we have a good awareness of who we are and our roles in the world.

More and more people are turning away from traditional social institutions like family hierarchies and religious communities. Because of this, we increasingly rely on the self as our primary source of identity, stability, and success. We may validate our individual selves through our careers, our possessions, or our romantic relationships. But deep down, we feel that we are the only ones responsible for our successes and failures.

Unfortunately, along with this mass of self-knowledge and self-sufficiency comes a mass of uncertainties. We start to question our abilities when we don't achieve the results we wanted. What if we're not as capable as our siblings at managing our careers or taking care of our family? What if our new friends judge us if they find out about the mistakes we made when we were younger? What if our partner falls out of love with us once we start to get wrinkles, gain weight, or make less money after tax? These "what ifs" form the basis of insecurity.

As the experts tell us, insecurity is the lack of confidence and certainty in yourself (Jacob, 2019; Vail et al., 1999). It fills your mind with fears, doubts, and worries that shape your thinking and lead to a progressively negative outlook towards life. This constant negativity makes you feel like you can't even cope with, let alone excel in your daily tasks. You try to hide these feelings at first. But over time, they become harder and harder to ignore.

"Insecurity is based on 0n negative thoughts that make us believe we are incapable, unworthy, or simply don't belong. These negative thoughts lead to negative feelings, which soon create negative habits (Hain, 2015a)."

These negative feelings quickly turn into negative actions. As a result, they prevent you from fitting into social groups, reaching your personal goals, and finding the support and acceptance that you need to be the best version of yourself.

Having insecurities is a normal part of being human. Most people have at least some areas of their life where they feel less confident than others. This includes anything from dancing in public to using a smartphone to solving simple math problems without a calculator. After all, nobody can be an expert at everything they do.

Just because you have a few insecurities doesn't mean that they automatically control your life. For example, you might not be able to dance. At your cousin's wedding, you might look enviously at your 90-year-old grandmother as she effortlessly keeps the beat to the Macarena. Meanwhile, you hide by the bar and hope that no one asks you why you're not joining. But you might also find some humor in the situation, laughing about it to your equally coordination-challenged uncle as you sip your drinks. You might remind yourself of the moving, well-written 'Congratulations' card you sent to the newlyweds. Or how you saved the day by catching the limo door just before it caught the bride's dress. Or how you made the 2000-mile trip across the country just to watch the groom make his vows to his true love. By not letting the insecurities get you down, you'll realize that there are more important things than knowing how to do a silly line dance. And you'll feel your fears and worries disappear, bit by bit.

But what if your insecurities are more severe than not knowing how to dance the Macarena? What if they're unending feelings of isolation and despair that are always at the back of your mind? What if they affect you in every area of your life, like your personal relationships, career, and the basic sense of well-being? What if they're increasing your anxiety or depression?

This is when our doubts and fears become the most devastating. But the good news is that you can master these more serious insecurities as well. Once you know the root causes of your insecurities, you can understand them, confront them, and tell them to get lost once and for all.

WHY DO WE FEEL INSECURE?

There are many reasons why we experience insecurity. We may be able to pin it to a specific traumatic incident. More likely, it's a combination of different events that slowly build up our fears and worries. We may not even be aware of some of these events, either because we were too young when they happened or because we didn't realize at the time that they were destructive. Especially when traumatic incidents repeat themselves, it's easy to normalize them and not understand how badly they affect our self-esteem.

Luckily, psychologists, life coaches, and other experts have some robust theories about the major causes of insecurity. These include hardwired thoughts, childhood trauma, distorted self-perception, and fears about the future.

Hardwired Thoughts

According to life coach Kate Romero, insecurities are behaviors that are either hardwired into your brain or picked up over time (cited in Jacob, 2019). Narcissists fall into this first category. Their minds are hardwired to make them feel inadequate, and they are terrified that others will find out about their low self-esteem. This is why narcissists are bullies. They overcompensate for their negative self-perceptions by making others feel bad about themselves. As

Romero notes, these hard-wired insecurities are extremely difficult to overcome.

Luckily, most people fall into the second category. Their insecurity wasn't hardwired from birth. Instead, it grew over time as they developed fears, anxieties, and doubts through everyday events. More often than not, these feelings appeared when they interacted with abusive, negligent, or overly critical people. Because of these interactions, they learned to view themselves and present themselves to the world as inferior and unworthy.

Learned insecurities are just as crappy to deal with as hardwired insecurities. Yet, unlike the hardwired type, they can be unlearned over time. Once you discover where your insecurities come from, you can take away their life-destroying power.

Past Experiences

Experts agree that childhood and early-adult experiences are the primary sources of fear, doubt, and worry (Jacob, 2019). After all, during this formative time, we learn the habits that will shape our adult life. We pick up these habits from our parents, caregivers, teachers, faith leaders, peers, friends, and romantic partners.

As babies and young children, we have a natural need for connection with our "attachment figures" (Becker-Phelps, 2016). These are older and wiser individuals, usually, our parents, who are emotionally available to take care of us.

They help us navigate life's problems, showing us what to do in stressful situations, how to manage our emotions, and how to build a successful life. Without our attachment figures, we would not be able to survive.

Yet, our parents and guardians aren't perfect. Whether intentional or not, they can make mistakes that fundamentally change the course of our adult life. They can transform us from being happy, hopeful, and self-assured kids to ones who need constant attention and validation from others.

"According to the experts, our insecurities mostly come from our childhood, through our interactions with our family, peers, teachers, or other mentors (Le Duc, 2016)."

According to psychologist Sal Raichbach and post-trauma coach Tonya McKenzie, your self-esteem is shaped by how your parents love you (cited in Jacob, 2019). If they shower you with love and affection, you will be more likely to grow into a satisfied, self-assured adult. If they deny you the love you need, you will be more likely to grow into an insecure, neurotic adult.

Even if you weren't abused as a child, you could still develop insecurities through tiny moments of neglect or criticism. For example, if your mother spends a lot of time on clothes and makeup, you might fear that you aren't attractive. You might think that if you were better looking, your mother would pay more attention to you instead. If this happens often enough, this insecurity will continue into your adult life, where you will continuously feel ugly and worthless.

You'll probably obsess over your appearance, devoting much of your time to following the latest clothing, hairstyle, facial hair, or makeup trends. This, in itself, may seem minor. But it can also translate into more dangerous habits, like diet pills, eating disorders, or cosmetic surgery.

Maybe your parents always gave you the love that you needed. But what if they didn't love themselves as strongly? Children internalize their parents' behaviors because it is their guideline for how to behave. Let's say your father is continually criticizing himself, saying that he's good for nothing and will never amount to anything. If you regularly hear these rants, you'll likely accept that this is a usual way to think about yourself. As an adult, you'll be just as self-critical as your father, nitpicking over your flaws and blaming your-self when things don't go according to plan.

In short, we make our own reality about who we are and how the world perceives us based on the type of love that exists in our childhood home. If we don't receive enough love from our parents or see enough self-love from our parents, we're more likely to develop fears, worries, and doubts that disrupt our everyday lives.

It's not just parental love that creates childhood insecurities. As Romero notes, it's also shaped by our interactions with classmates, teachers, clergy, or other authority figures (cited in Jacob 2019). Especially as older children, we tend to spend more time away from our parents. Instead, we seek mean-ingful connections with friends and mentors. Trying to fit in with a group at school and being told you don't belong can be just as devastating on your self-esteem as having unloving parents. You will carry this sense of not belonging to your adult life, where you will feel anxious in different social situations.

A similar thing happens when you try to learn a new skill, like drawing pictures, playing soccer, or interpreting sacred texts. If you're criticized continuously when trying to learn these skills, you'll only become more self-conscious about your abilities. You'll give up on your lessons, feeling stupid and useless. You'll even shy away from trying new things in your adult life, for fear of criticism.

Let's say you had a supportive childhood. Your parents gave you the love you needed and set a positive example for you to learn how to love yourself. You found a reliable group of friends to help you navigate the angst and drama of growing up. You were guided by your mentors to reach your full academic, artistic, and spiritual potentials. But then you meet your first romantic partner. And suddenly, all those painstaking efforts to build up your self-esteem go out the window.

Christianne Kernes, therapist, and co-founder of the *LARKR* mental-health app, argues that past relationships can profoundly affect your insecurities (cited in Jacob, 2019). If an ex-partner broke your trust during that relationship, if they were unfaithful or abandoned you for someone else, you may fear that you are not good enough for your future partners. This fear leads to many types of insecure behavior. You may be overly critical of your physical appearance, always ask your partners to confirm that they love you, or act jealous when your partner spends time with other people.

These insecurities become even worse in a physically or verbally abusive relationship. As adults, our romantic partners become our attachment figures (Becker-Phelps, 2016). We can survive without them, but they become such a crucial part of our identity that we try to hold onto the relationship as best we can. Even when your partner doesn't give you the love we deserve, you may still feel you cannot make it through your life without them. The longer you stay, the more you suffer abuse, the more your insecurities grow, and the more you think that maybe you do deserve to suffer, for whatever reason. This makes it more difficult for you to finally leave and find someone who will treat you properly. It becomes a vicious cycle that's only broken once you realize why your insecurity exists and how it affects you.

It doesn't matter whether it comes from parents, peers, or partners—if we are made to feel worthless regularly, we will carry these feelings with us. Over time, these negative thoughts become ingrained in our heads, affecting our beliefs about ourselves and our capabilities.

Critical Beliefs About Ourselves

Life coach Lisa Philyaw and wellness expert Caleb Backe argue that insecurity comes from the relationship you create with yourself (cited in Jacob, 2019). It depends on how you perceive yourself and present that perception of the world. If you have negative thoughts about your worth and abilities, you will be more likely to internalize those thoughts as beliefs. When you do, your self-perception matters more than the actual reality.

"When we are insecure, we constantly judge and belittle ourselves. We become our own worst critics (Altmann, 2017)."

For example, let's say that you don't know how to master a new computer program at work. If all your coworkers seem to manage quite easily, you may blame yourself for struggling to keep up. Even if your boss or coworkers don't say anything about it, the little voice in your head that telling you you're stupid makes the pain feel just as real as if someone said it out loud. Of course, if your boss does tell you that you're incompetent, it only reinforces the negative thoughts that exist in your mind. This criticism becomes even more painful if it's something you've never considered. You may have criticized yourself for not mastering that specific program. But you may not have assumed that you're incompetent at everything you do. As a result, you gain new insecurities that never existed before.

As you continue to face new challenges, you will keep reminding yourself of these negative thoughts every time you fail to meet the expectations of others or yourself. You become too harsh on yourself, ignoring your successes and focusing only on your real or perceived failures.

When you accept that insecurities are normal feelings that everyone experiences from time to time, you can courageously tell them to fuck off, knowing that they don't define who you are. You recognize them as harmful, uncertain thoughts that have nothing at all to do with your worth or abilities. So, even if you don't perform quite as well as you expected, you can still pick yourself up and try to do better next time.

Yet, when you accept your insecurities as an unchangeable reflection of who you are, you only feel worse about yourself (Jacob, 2019). As I mentioned before, negative thoughts lead to negative beliefs, which quickly lead to negative actions. Once you get in the habit of believing the worst about yourself, you externalize these beliefs and mistake them for your reality. You fail to see negative thoughts for what they are—just thoughts. Instead, they feel like unchangeable, universal truths.

Some people are upfront about their insecure feelings and allow them to guide their actions. They are so overcome by their critical beliefs that they become an inescapable habit. Others try to hide their beliefs away and pretend like they don't exist. As we'll see in Chapter 9, this defense mechanism will eventually backfire. The longer you spend trying to bottle-up negative emotions, the more likely they will explode out of you at unexpected times. Unable to return to your pretense that everything is normal, you will become like the first group of insecure people, displaying your fears and doubts for everyone to see and guide your life.

You may even prefer this loss of control to agonize over your future.

Uncertainty About the Future

Paul Levin, a motivational speaker and founder of *I Deserve a Perfect Life*, states that insecurity comes from fears about the future (cited in Jacob, 2019). As I said before, insecurities are based on "what ifs." When it seems like our personal or professional lives are no longer as stable as they once were, we start to imagine different future outcomes to regain that sense of control. We try to protect ourselves from disappointment by imagining the worst-case scenario. When we let these negative predictions control our minds, we have no hope that things will work out for us. We only strengthen our doubts about our abilities.

Levin also notes that our beliefs about the future tend to come true, according to our perceptions. If we have positive beliefs about our worth and capabilities, then we will be able to confidently handle whatever the future brings us, even if it's something unpleasant. If we have negative beliefs about our worth and capabilities, then we won't be able to deal with whatever the future brings us. Even if something pleasant happens, we will be suspicious of it, because it doesn't match our expectations. We will keep waiting for something to go wrong and fulfill our insecure predictions.

Whether or not your insecurities come from hardwired thoughts, past experiences, critical beliefs about yourself, uncertainties about the future, or a combination of any of the above, they all produce the same effect. They make you uncertain about your abilities and doubtful of your inherent self-worth. They make you feel uneasy and anxious, even if you have no logical reason to feel that way. They make your negative self-perceptions more critical than the actual reality. But most importantly, they don't have to be permanent.

Now that you know your insecurities and where they come from, you're ready to confront them and take back control of your life.

Throughout this book, you will be guided through different kinds of insecurities. You'll be given the tools to handle them and receive answers to all your questions. By telling your insecurities to fuck off, so you'll achieve the happiness and confidence you've always wanted.

Let's get started by looking at two of the most common forms of insecurity: comparison and jealousy.

2

COMPARISON AND JEALOUSY

D o you always fear the people or things you care about will be taken from you? Are you still judging others to make yourself feel superior? Do you measure your successes and failures against other people's successes and failures? If you answered yes to any of these, you have one of two interconnected insecurities: comparison and jealousy.

Comparison happens when you measure your abilities, relationships, or possessions against others, taking careful note of the similarities and differences (Bacon, 2014; Brown, 2010; Swan, n.d.). You position yourself as superior, inferior, or equal, depending on the standards that you set for yourself or that others set for you. This includes family members, friends, neighbors, coworkers, and anyone else you regularly interact with. It can also happen on a societal level when you come face to face with expectations about how you should live your life.

Comparing yourself to others can be a useful tool for friendly competition. It encourages you to do your best. Yet, it is destructive when it's always nagging at the back of your mind. If it never goes away, the comparison makes you feel anxious, unworthy, and overall insecure about your abilities.

"If left unchecked, comparison and jealousy can turn everything into a competition, where we always come out as the losers (Socha, 2016)."

Jealousy is a specific type of comparison, where you believe you are in danger of losing something important to you to another person or an activity (Lamia, 2013; Swan, n.d.). It's a normal emotion that everyone experiences from time to time. But when you're always worried about losing friends to other friends or having someone upstage you in theatre production, this is when jealousy becomes problematic. It makes you question your worth, causing you to feel inferior to the person or activity that you see as your threat. You may fill the void by being judgmental and hoping this makes you feel superior.

Another closely related form of comparison is envy. Unlike jealousy, envy is focused on gaining something from another person. Yet, it can lead to similar judgmental behavior, where you try to suppress your inferior feelings by belittling someone based on their relationships, possessions, or abilities.

Comparison-based insecurities come from several sources, including social media, early childhood experiences, and traumatic relationships. Once you know where you picked up your negative habits, you can start clearing your mind of crappy comparisons, replacing them with self-assured generosity and empathy.

WHY WE HAVE IT

Comparison and jealousy reflect our deepest desires (Swan, n.d.). They remind us of the relationships, possessions, or qualities that we don't have, think we don't have, or are in danger of losing. These absences bother us at a deep, personal level and lower our self-esteem. This is why Bacon (2014) calls comparison "part ego ... part creative drive ... part deep soul yearning" (n.p.).

Many people blame modern media on these insecurities. It's true that social media and celebrity culture encourage us to compare ourselves to others (Bacon, 2014; Brown, 2007; Hopper, 2019). You may scroll through your Instagram feed and wonder why you don't seem as beautiful, perfect, or successful as influencers and celebrities. But people only present the most exciting, glamorous, and dramatic aspects of their lives. They gloss over ordinary activities, like buying food, filing tax returns, or taking the dog for a \

walk. They also don't show us the behind-the-scenes work that goes into building their brand, so it seems like they are just naturally talented at what they do. This way, we always feel 'boring' compared to people who always seem to be traveling to exciting places, attending fancy parties, or doing other 'extraordinary' things.

However, for most people, the roots of their insecurities run a lot deeper than new media. After all, people had struggled with them long before Mark Zuckerberg and the Kardashians ever existed. This is because comparison and jealousy are rooted in shame, which is an effect, or biological reaction to our emotions.

A big part of your sense of self comes from comparing yourself to the idea of who you want to be (Lamia, 2013). Your role model might be a celebrity. But more often than not, it's someone that can see your successes and failures firsthand. When you fail to match the ideal that they have set, you feel ashamed. Jealousy and envy are two products of this shame. You fear you have lost your role model's respect and try your hardest to gain it back.

Like other insecurities, comparison and jealousy are often learned in childhood, when we don't receive enough attention or praise from our parents. Because of this neglect and criticism, we compare ourselves unfavorably to others or feel threatened when something tries to take attention away from us.

Let's say that you grew up with an older brother who was a straight-A student, while you struggled in school. Your parents always praised your brother and asked you why you couldn't be more like him. Because of this, you ever felt like the inferior sibling. As an adult, you'll be more likely to belittle your accomplishments and compare yourself unfavorably to others. To save yourself from these envious feelings, you might also belittle your brother's accomplishments or nitpick at other aspects of his life. By being judgmental, you're trying to save yourself from the shame of not living up to your parents' standards.

Even when our parents don't explicitly criticize us, similar things can happen when they don't give us enough attention. Let's say that your parents divorced when you were young. After the divorce, your mother went through a series of relationships where she paid more attention to her new partners than you. From a young age, you learned to see these romantic partners as rivals for your mother's care. And, they were usually more successful than you at capturing it. Because you felt neglected as a child, you'll obsessively seek attention from others as an adult. This will translate into your own romantic relationships, where you continuously worry the relationship is under threat whenever your partner doesn't give you the attention you crave (Becker-Phelps, 2016; Jacob, 2019). As a result, you become jealous whenever they spend time with other people or don't invite you to join activities.

Jealousy doesn't always start at home. We can also develop it later in life through our romantic relationships. This is especially common with people who are brand new to dating and don't know how to act in a relationship. It also shows up in people who have had unfaithful partners break their trust by being absent or unfaithful.

No matter what time of life it happens, uncontrolled jealousy wreaks havoc on relationships by encouraging your negative habits. You might become angry and fight with the person who you think is 'stealing' your partner (Becker-Phelps, 2016; Lamia, 2013). You might try to control your partner to prevent them from abandoning you. You might become more distant, hoping that your partner will notice and make more effort to make you feel valued and secure. You might become judgmental, belittling your partners' friends and hobbies to remind them that you are the most important thing in their life.

When you feel insecure about your ability to live up to your standards or maintain meaningful relationships, you mistakenly believe that you can escape these pressures by being judgmental (Brown, 2007). Even if you don't say it in words, you can still make your judgments known by your body language and tone of voice. No matter how you express it, judgmental behavior is a dangerous side effect. By trying to make yourself superior, you make others think less of you. As a result, you risk losing essential relationships with the people you care about. For example, your constant criticism will alienate you from your brother, while your jealous behavior will end your romantic relationship.

So, what can you do about these insecurities? Fortunately, there are several tried and true methods for overcoming comparison and jealousy, as we'll see in the next section.

HOW WE CAN OVERCOME IT

The most natural solution may seem to tell yourself to stop comparing yourself to others. If only it were that easy! Empty words don't stop us from feeling how we feel or act the way we act (Swan, n.d.). Plus, it only makes us feel more ashamed of ourselves and more likely to become jealous and judgmental.

Instead, detach yourself from the situation. Think about why you feel the need to compare yourself to others. Take note of the root causes outlined in the last section. Then, start experimenting with the solutions mentioned below. Soon, you'll be able to tell your comparisons and jealousy to fuck off, so you can earn back your self-confidence.

Be Honest

Whenever you start to compare yourself to others or worry about losing a meaningful relationship, the worst thing you can do is deny these feelings. When we bottle up our negative emotions and pretend they don't exist, they have a way of exploding out of us at moments when we don't expect them to (Becker-Phelps, 2016). Acknowledge your comparisons and jealousies as soon as they come up. This way, you can find the right solutions before they get out of hand.

We can't just be honest with ourselves about our comparisons and jealousies. We also have to be honest with others.

Sometimes, they don't realize that their words and actions hurt us. For example, your parents may have thought that by comparing you to your brother, they would encourage you to work harder at school. If you explain how their comparisons made you feel, they might realize that what they did was wrong and apologize for it. Even if they don't, you'll still feel a lot better about the situation by talking about it than keeping it inside.

You can take a similar approach with your brother. Explain to him that you've always envied him because of how your parents treated him. You might be surprised to learn that it made him feel uncomfortable, too, especially when you took out your resentment on him. Again, even if your brother is not responsive, you will still feel better for reaching out to him to try to make peace.

Similarly, when jealousy starts to fuck up your romantic relationship, be honest with your partner, and calmly explain why you feel jealous (Jacob, 2019). Together, you can find a solution where you can both feel at ease in the relationship. If your partner is unsupportive, you can look for someone else who will make you feel secure and valued (Lamia, 2013).

Once you are honest about how you feel, you'll free yourself from the endless need to compare yourself to others or fear to lose the things you care about. Instead, you'll learn to see things from a healthier perspective.

Connect, Don't Compare

As Swan (n.d.) says, comparison and jealousy are an unfair game because we "[compare] the worst we know about ourselves to the best we assume about others" (n.p.). Whenever we do this, we always come out as the loser. Instead, we should look for healthier ways to view our personal qualities and relationships. This way, we can recognize ourselves for the winners that we are. How do we do this? By connecting to our own strengths and building empathetic relationships with other people.

The best way to do this is to remind yourself that everyone is unique. No one is good at everything, but everyone excels at something. Albert Einstein may not have said the famous quote that Kelly (2004) attributes to him. But it doesn't make it any less real that "if you judge a fish by its ability to climb a tree, it will live its whole life believing that it is stupid" (p. 82).

Instead of focusing on what you aren't able to do, focus on all the things that you can do. Connect to your talents and celebrate your accomplishments, no matter how small. With this positive outlook, you won't need to compare yourself unfavorably to others.

Similarly, you can play what Swan (n.d.) calls "the game of abundance." Instead of focusing on the skills, you think you lack, think of all the ways that you have those skills. For example, if you feel you are not as smart as your older brother, think about the topics you know a lot about. They don't even have to be academic subjects. They might be anything from cooking fancy dinners to editing podcasts to repairing broken gadgets. Once you connect to your strengths, you'll realize that you have your own unique form of intelligence, even if it doesn't match your brother's type.

When you're in the habit of comparing yourself to others, it's tempting to oversimplify things (Bacon, 2014; Swan, n.d.). You might assume that they achieve more than you do because they are inherently better than you. But this is false thinking. You need to recognize that you don't know everything about the person you're comparing yourself to. You have no idea what they had to go through to achieve the position they're in.

For example, your older brother probably had to work hard to achieve all those As. You may not have noticed all the studying he did while you were busy playing video games or jogging outside. He probably had to sacrifice a lot of things that you benefited from, like spending more time with friends, participating in extracurricular activities, or even trying new hobbies. Just because you never noticed the hard work that he put in doesn't mean that it was easy for him to get good grades.

This is one of those times when positive comparison might work to your advantage. Pay attention to how the people you envy achieve their successes. Ask your brother how he studied, how often he studied, what he thought he did well, and what he wishes to do better. By connecting to other people instead of comparing yourself against them, you can motivate yourself to reach your own goals and learn new skills along the way.

Connection can also help you overcome jealousy. Don't eliminate the 'threat.' Instead, use uncertainty as an excuse to develop an even stronger bond with the person you care about. For example, don't try to stop your partner from spending time with their friends. Ask them to set aside another day when you can see each other. Try a new class at the gym, check out a restaurant that you haven't been to in a while, or get to know them better over a game of "Would You Rather." By focusing on strengthening your relationship with your partner, you'll be less likely to worry about losing them.

"Connection and empathy are two of the best solutions for overcoming jealousy and comparison (LinkedIn Sales Navigator, 2017)."

Empathy is the key to building successful connections with others (Brown, 2007). By fully engaging with others and seeing things from their point of view, you save yourself from feeling ashamed and becoming judgmental. Instead, you realize that the people you see as 'threats' are just like you––flawed, unsure at times, but in need of support and compassion.

When you focus on connecting instead of comparing, you'll increase your sense of self-worth. This way, it will be much easier to say goodbye to your unfavorable thoughts and beliefs.

Become Better, Not Bitter

Whenever we feel threatened by comparison or jealousy, it's easy to wallow in self-pity. But with the right mindset, it can be just as easy to use your insecurities to become a better version of yourself.

How can you do this? By forming connections. This not only encourages you to think positively. It also helps you develop skills you never thought you'd have otherwise.

Whenever you're feeling envious, dare yourself to reach the level of the other person (Bacon, 2014). Take full advantage of positive comparison. Let's say that because of your older brother's school smarts, he's now a successful family doctor. You could use his success story to motivate yourself to achieve more in your own career. Play a more active role in meetings. Take on new projects. Research new techniques related to your career field. Who knows? You may even get promoted.

You could also use your brother's success as an excuse to learn something new. Talk to him about his job. Ask him everything you've always wanted to know about medicine. By expanding your knowledge, you'll feel less inferior to your brother. You'll build a better relationship with him, based on sharing knowledge instead of sharing insults.

Another effective strategy to fight comparison is to channel that energy into getting creative (Brown, 2010). Creativity is an expression of our own individual style and power. By doing creative things like sculpting, writing poetry, playing an instrument, or shooting videos, you get in touch with the weird and wonderful things that make you who you are. You'll express the best version of yourself, even if it's not what others expect of you.

Make Positive Pain Your Friend

You are still feeling the need to compare and judge, even after you bought a craft kit and tried a HIIT class with your partner? You may want to fight comparison and jealousy the old-fashioned way through negative reinforcement. This is a conditioning method that encourages you to act a certain way by avoiding negative consequences when you operate in the opposite direction (Iwata, 1987).

I used to do the trick with myself, where every time I started to feel jealous or started to compare myself to others, I had to punish myself by doing something I didn't like. Sometimes I did five push-ups. Sometimes I gave $5 to a friend. Over time, I became more aware each time I had a negative thought. To give my arms a break and protect my life savings, I learned to avoid those negative feelings. As a result, I started to feel a lot more confident about my abilities.

Swan (n.d.) argues that giving money to a friend has other benefits as well since it encourages you to be generous.

When you focus more on giving than getting, it becomes harder to feel jealous or envious. Over time, these positive actions turn into positive habits. In a way, this is a positive reinforcement, where you try to maximize the good feeling of being generous in attempting to give as much as you can.

Whether it's reinforcements, building empathetic connections, and/or improving your skills, you'll be able to find the right solution for you once you are honest about your tendency to compare yourself to others or be jealous of them. Try a couple of different ones out and see what works best for you. Soon, you'll start feeling those insecurities disappear. You'll replace them with a belief in your abilities and a strong sense of stability in your personal relationships.

But what if you always feel like you're not enough, even when you're not comparing yourself to others? What if it's your insecurities themselves that make you feel insecure? Don't worry: I'll cover this feeling of unworthiness in the next chapter.

3

NOT BEING ENOUGH

S ometimes our insecurities aren't based just on how we compare and contrast ourselves to others. Instead, they can be deep-rooted personal beliefs about what we are like as individuals. These insecurities come from that little voice that fucks up your head, filling it with negative thoughts about your abilities.

In moderation, this inner critic has its benefits (Guay, 2018). It guides you out of trouble, keeps you modest, and encourages you to do our best. But when you're always telling yourself that you're never good enough, this inner voice does more harm than good. Without a muzzle, it can destroy your self-esteem.

Feeling like you can never do anything right is one of the crappiest experiences. In a way, it makes you feel insecure about your insecurities. This double-threat to your sense of self stops you from valuing who you are and recognizing that you're still worthy, even though you're not perfect.

How can you get rid of this feeling? First, you need to identify where the problem comes from. Once you know why you feel unworthy, you can mastermind a plan to start feeling comfortable in your own skin and regain the confidence you deserve.

WHY WE HAVE IT

Like comparison and jealousy, the insecurity of not enough coming from that shame effect we talked about in Chapter 2 (Guay, 2018). When you feel unworthy, you're hyperconscious about how other people perceive you. You often think you're being watched and judged by others, even when they don't seem to be paying attention to you. This is a harmful cycle that makes you feel ashamed when you don't live up to the expectations you set for yourself. Even when you're the only one who's being critical, the pain feels just as real as if it were coming from another person.

"When we feel like we're not enough, we become our own worst critics, filling our minds with fears and doubts (Hain, 2015b)."

Unworthiness can come from several sources. Social media has a knack for bringing out our inner critic. It makes you feel like you always have to present a perfect image to your followers, even when you're secretly unsure of yourself and worry that you're not attractive/intelligent/funny/interesting enough. Still, these feelings usually predate our Twitter accounts. They often take root in childhood, choking out the naturally positive beliefs we have about our personalities, looks, and abilities.

More often than not, when you feel like you're not enough, it's because of traumas you experienced either at home or at school. As I mentioned in Chapter 2, we tend to internalize whatever our parents and peers tell us. And when they continuously focus on the negative, we learn to do the same.

Let's say your father had an unconventional way to stop you from misbehaving in public. Instead of trying to reason with you and explain why your actions were wrong, he would simply say, "Don't do that or people won't like you." He may not have meant any harm by it. He probably only said that to get you to think about others' feelings whenever you had a screaming match at the park or threw food at a restaurant. Still, because your father referenced other people's judgments when correcting your behavior, you learned to become overly concerned about what others think of you. As an adult, you always worry that people won't like you if you make mistakes. You hide your faults and weaknesses. You hope that if you ignore them long enough, they'll disappear on their own. But they still nag at your psyche, as you fail to live up to the expectation of being perfect and likable at all times.

Even worse, negative beliefs tend to be passed down in a snowball effect (Rudolph, 2017). They become even stronger and more destructive with each generation. Let's say that your father grew up with parents who lived through World War II. During the war, your grandparents had to learn to make sacrifices for the greater good of society. Because of this, your father may have learned to devalue self-love, mistaking it for selfishness. When he passed this 'selfless' worldview on to you, he added to it by telling you not to show negative emotions in public so that you wouldn't upset other people. You might then pass this on to your kids in an even more extreme form, telling them not to show any emotions at all. As you can see, it's easy for these unworthy feelings to grow out of control if they're left untreated.

Even if your home was a welcoming and supportive environment, you could still learn to feel unworthy at school. Maybe you had a toxic friend who always put you down. At recess, she would laugh at you whenever you fumbled over a soccer ball. She would take over group projects, telling you that she was better at making posters or speaking in front of the class. She would never come to play at your house because she said she had better toys at her home. In this case, you might start assuming that you're inferior in every part of your life. Even if you eventually fall out and start spending time with better friends, you can easily carry those negative feelings into adulthood, continually doubting your ability to work, parent, or excel at new activities.

Unworthiness can also arise in adulthood when we meet people who think or do things differently from us. They may explicitly judge us for being different. Or, we might judge ourselves for failing to think or act in the same way. For example, you might start a new marketing job where your boss expects you to work rapidly to meet strict deadlines. By contrast, you might feel you do your best work at a slower pace, taking the time to fix small details and look everything over before submitting your presentations. There's nothing inherently wrong with either method. But by not meeting your boss's expectations, you might feel like you can't do your job correctly. This can quickly extend into other areas of your life, where you doubt your intelligence, problem-solving skills, or general self-worth.

No matter where it comes from, unworthiness is a deep-rooted belief that fundamentally shapes the way you think about yourself. It makes you feel like being enough is something you have to earn instead of something you automatically have (Camara Wilkins, 2017). It closes your mind to all of your amazing qualities and abilities, so you can only focus on your fears and failures (Chen, 2018). It teaches you to hide your true self in order to fit into the social role you think you're supposed to fill (Branden, 1988). This creates inner turmoil, where you lose contact with who you really are and continuously fail at trying to be someone else.

The good news is that unworthiness doesn't have to be a permanent condition. Once you understand that these negative perceptions really are just negative perceptions, you can look past your insecurities and realize that you were wrong––you were enough all along.

HOW WE CAN OVERCOME IT

Again, overcoming deep-rooted insecurity isn't as simple as waking up one day and saying you're not going to feel a certain way anymore. It's a difficult journey that requires a daily commitment to confronting your worst beliefs about yourself and working hard to turn them into positive self-love messages.

By getting to know your wants and desires, practicing self-care, facing your fears of failure, questioning perfectionism, and connecting with your authentic self, you'll be able to feel those doubts disappear. Instead, you'll be filled with unshakeable self-worth.

Get to Know Yourself

When you're always focused on your shortcomings, it's easy to forget who you are at that fundamental level, beyond your insecurities. Over time, your wants, desires, hopes, and dreams may become alien to you (Chen, 2018; Guay, 2018). But by making a conscious effort to connect with them, you'll regain that positive sense of self that motivates you to live your best life. You'll be much happier by directing your-self to the life you want to live instead of hating yourself for being stuck in a life that you hate.

Your inner critic will try its hardest to tell you that you don't deserve this life. Each time it does, tell that little voice to shut the hell up. Direct your attention to something that you like about yourself. For example, instead of criticizing your slow speed at work, remind yourself how much your last client appreciated the extra time and effort you spent on the strategy guidelines for their brand. Or how much your boss praised your PowerPoint proofreading skills at your last meeting. Then, challenge yourself to think of more strengths that you bring to the workplace. These might be anything from a well-organized desk to a good sense of humor to an uncanny ability to fix whatever's wrong with the Nespresso machine.

By focusing on your positive qualities, you'll realize that you aren't as flawed as you think. As Jon Kabat-Zinn says, "As long as you are breathing, there is more right with you than wrong with you, no matter how ill or how despairing you may feel in a given moment" (2013, p. 89).

"Getting in touch with who you open the path to self-love and accepting all your imperfections (LaRue, 2017)."

Another easy way to get to know your good qualities is to have conversations with others (Guay, 2018). As you open up and share positive facts about yourself, you'll start to recognize that people care more about these than whatever faults you think you might have. You'll not only build healthier relationships. You'll also give your self-esteem a much-needed boost by reminding yourself of all you have to offer.

Practice Self-Care

As Guay (2018) argues, self-love and self-care go hand in hand. Eating healthy, exercising regularly, and getting enough sleep is just as crucial for your mental health as your physical health. This way, it will be much easier to boost your mood and keep a positive outlook on life.

This doesn't mean that you should spend loads of money on bath bombs, mindful coloring books, or other self-care gimmicks (Rudolph, 2018). It's all about finding the right way to unwind from your daily stresses and meet your needs. Whether it's listening to your favorite podcast, doing an at-home workout, or meditating with essential oils, you can find the right feel-good activities to help you feel less anxious about who you are and what you have to offer.

By making a conscious effort to take care of yourself, you'll feel a lot better about your strengths and weaknesses. And by loving who you are, you'll take better care of yourself. It's a positive feedback loop that will propel you to new heights as you work to overcome your feelings of not being worthy.

Face Your Fears

Whenever you feel uncertain about your abilities, it's tempting to endlessly postpone unpleasant things until you feel like you're ready to face them (Chen, 2018; Davret,

2019; Guay, 2018). Yet, if you keep leaving problems for your future self to deal with, you never give yourself the chance to overcome them. And you'll only keep feeling like you aren't capable enough to handle whatever difficulties come your way.

Facing your fears is scary as hell. But you have to be willing to take significant risks to get big rewards. You'll feel a lot more confident about these risks if you let go of your 'shoulds' and turn them into 'cans' and 'wills.'

Let's say your friend has been begging you to come to the weekly yoga class that he teaches. You want to support your friend, but you're worried that you're not athletic enough. It's tempting to channel your toxic childhood friend's voice, telling you that you shouldn't make a fool of yourself in a room full of super flexible strangers. But instead, try focusing on what you can do. You can attend the class, even if you don't master the poses and everyone else. You will still learn from your mistakes and be able to use them to do better next time. You may even surprise yourself by what your body can do when you give it a chance. By focusing on the power of your choices instead of your negative expectations, you'll empower yourself to try new things and accomplish new feats.

Still, having trouble moving yourself to action? Don't be afraid to reach out for help and encouragement. For example, if you ask your friend to teach you some of the poses before the class, you might feel less self-conscious about giving yoga a try. Like Camara Wilkins (2017) says, being enough doesn't mean you're completely self-sufficient. It means being aware of your capabilities and your needs and recognizing that you aren't perfect.

Be Skeptical About Perfectionism

As we learned in Chapter 2, people love to exaggerate things to make themselves feel superior. So be cautious about accepting everything you hear as the ultimate truth (Chen, 2018). Nothing is as ideal as they seem.

In Western society, we're constantly bombarded with tips and tricks on living a perfect life. They're supposed to lead us to the same outcome––working a well-paid 9-to-5 job, then spending our weekends in a huge suburban house with our beautiful partner, 2.3 kids, and loyal golden retriever.

Yet, even when you achieve that 'perfect' life, it's easy to feel like you're barely keeping everything together. This is because no matter how hard we try to be perfect, we all have flaws. We have rough days at work. We fight with our partners. We make mistakes with our kids. We even forget to walk the dog. We're only human, after all.

When you obsess over keeping up a perfect facade, you're not only trying to do the impossible. At the heart of the matter, you're trying to be someone that you're not. You're doing this because you think the real you is unacceptable.

Instead of telling yourself that you aren't good enough, embrace everything that you are, despite your imperfections.

Being upfront about your flaws will free you from the need to be perfect and give you the freedom to be you. As a result, you'll start feeling a lot more comfortable about who you are and what you're capable of.

It's also important not to blow your faults out of proportion. Remind yourself that you are more than your mistakes. For example, just because you lost your temper with your daughter doesn't make you a bad parent. It definitely doesn't mean that she'll hate you for it. It just means that you made a mistake. Apologize to your daughter, then brainstorm ways you can express your anger more constructively. By accepting your flaws and learning from them, you can use them to inspire you to do better (Davret, 2019). This way, you'll be another step closer to telling your inner critic to shut up once and for all.

Being enough means you don't have to prove yourself to anyone, especially your inner critic (Camara Wilkins, 2017). It means you can keep growing and learning in order to become the best version of yourself. Not a perfect version. But one that's authentically you.

Be Authentic

According to Branden (1988), part of growing up in our society is accepting that lying is a normal part of life. We always have to lie about who we truly are to fit in with our friends, coworkers, and neighbors on the other side of that white picket fence. But 'belonging' and 'being' are polar opposites of each other. We can't be ourselves if we're too caught up with trying to belong in our social groups.

To overcome your feelings of not being enough, you can't just acknowledge your strengths and weaknesses in private. You need to embrace your authentic self publicly. This means not only getting to know yourself but sharing who you are with the world around you.

To help you become more authentic, he suggests writing six to ten endings for the following statements (p.179):

"The hard thing about being honest with myself about what I'm feeling is _____."

"The hard thing about being honest with others about my feelings is _____."

"If I strived to be true and accurate in my communications _____."

Don't hold anything back––just be honest and write down whatever comes to mind. You might surprise yourself by how easily the answers come to you.

Complete this exercise every day for two months. Over time, connecting to these thoughts will come more naturally to you. By the end, you won't only be writing solutions to your insecurities. You'll be putting them into action and seeing positive results.

Many people think that authenticity is something you have when actually, it's something you choose to be (Brown,

2010). By choosing to let go of who you're supposed to be and embrace who you really are, you'll learn that your authentic self is more than enough. This will raise your self-esteem, increase your happiness, and encourage you to seek healthier relationships with yourself and with other people.

No one can entirely escape the voice of that inner critic. Everyone has days where they feel like they're not performing at their best. The important thing is that you don't let these insecurities control your life or make you doubt all the amazing imperfections that make you who you are.

But what if feeling enough isn't enough for you? What if you find yourself slipping back into self-doubt as soon as you go out into the social jungle, looking to others to validate your worth instead of finding it within yourself? If this is the case, your insecurities run a lot deeper than feeling unworthy, as we'll see in the next chapter.

4

VALIDATION

E verybody needs to feel good about themselves. It's one of those core emotional needs we automatically turn to after our physical needs for food, water, and shelter are met (Suval, 2012). Unless we feel safe and secure, we never find that inner peace we crave.

But we don't always look inside ourselves to satisfy this need (Geddis, 2018; Strauss Cohen, 2018). After all, soul searching takes a lot of time and effort. It's a path filled with self-doubt. It's quicker and easier to look outside ourselves to other people for this feel-good dopamine rush. When others approve of us, we feel like we can do anything. But when they don't, we feel like our world is falling apart. This insecurity is a trademark sign of validation.

To a certain extent, it's reasonable to care what people think, especially if they're people you care about (Nair, 2013; Varshika G, 2019). If you didn't, you would be a sociopath.

Plus, without consulting others, you wouldn't be able to discover new ways of doing things. You wouldn't be able to recognize the potential pros and cons of your actions without picking other brains.

But validation is like a drug. If you are addicted, it's easy to lose control over your life by living for the high of others' approval (Buckley, 2018; Strauss, Cohen 2018). And what used to make you feel good about yourself starts to make you feel shitty. You become powerless to make decisions without checking in with others first. You become paralyzed in your comfort zone, unable to achieve your goals and dreams. Your performance at school and work goes down. Worst of all, your stress levels skyrocket, leading to all sorts of health problems.

How can you tell if your approval-seeking behavior crosses the line? Uniacke (2018) and Buckley (2018) provide some common warning signs. These include:

Being a people-pleaser: Whatever you do is motivated by how other people feel about it. You go to extreme lengths to make everyone happy, even when you're secretly miserable.

Avoiding conflict at all costs: To you, there's nothing worse than conflict. You sacrifice your core beliefs to fit in with the crowd, and you soften your opinions when people challenge them. You take the blame when anything goes wrong, even when you have nothing to apologize for.

Overreacting to criticism: You take it personally when people disagree with you. You see criticism as a personal failure instead of an opportunity to improve.

Being a doormat: You have no idea how to say 'no.' You overcommit to things so people will like you, even when you're exhausted. You also don't stand up for yourself when others take advantage of you.

Gossiping: You enjoy being the center of attention and try to impress others with your insider knowledge––even when it's hurtful or untrue.

Passive aggressiveness: You always complain about how people treat you, but you never confront them. This extends outside your personal life too. When you're at a restaurant, you don't let them know when their service is poor. You also don't request refunds when you receive the wrong item you ordered or receive one that doesn't work correctly.

Faking knowledge: Even when you don't know anything about a subject, you pretend you do so that you won't seem stupid.

Fishing for compliments: You give people compliments when you don't mean them and try to get compliments when you don't earn them. You get easily frustrated when your plans fail, or when others brush off your compliments or don't return them.

Rebelling for attention: Maybe you really are a nonconformist at heart, and you're just true to yourself. Or maybe you just want others to think you're cool by piercing your eyebrow or experimenting with hallucinogenic drugs.

Like other forms of insecurity, the best way to cure yourself of validation is to identify its causes, then find the solutions that work for you. This way, you'll empower yourself to make your own decisions, celebrate your own accomplishments, and feel confident in your abilities.

WHY WE HAVE IT

On a basic level, validation is a sign of low self-esteem (Geddis, 2018; Uniacke, 2018). Some people are naturally self-critical and need that extra vote of confidence from people they care about. It might even be genetic, especially if your parents show approval-seeking behaviors. Still, most experts agree that we pick up validation as a learned behavior. We usually get it from people who have an enormous influence on us, whether it's close family members, friends, or other authority figures.

As children, we have an innate need to receive our parents' approval (Suval, 2012). If we don't, it only makes us more desperate to earn it. Let's say your mother was overly critical of you. She never gave compliments, but would always nitpick over your grades, clothes, hobbies, and friend group. At your hockey games, she would scream directions at you from the stands and ask why you didn't shoot the puck when she told you to or why the coach never picked you for MVP. At your violin recitals, she would take note of every mistake you made then make you practice for hours at home until you got it right. Because of her behavior, you felt like you could never do anything right. But you would still push yourself to your limits, desperately hoping to hear her say she was proud of you. As an adult, you'll be less likely to believe in your worth and abilities unless you listen to it from others.

You can also seek validation when you're told not to express yourself (Buckley, 2018). Let's say you had trouble making friends at school because you were obsessed with dinosaurs. Whenever you'd talk about velociraptors or bring out your fossil dig kit, other kids would make fun of you for being 'weird.' They refused to eat lunch with you, play with you at recess, or be your partner in group projects. As a result, you learned to keep your dinosaur passion for yourself. This self-conscious behavior will carry into your adult years, where you hide your true self to avoid criticism.

Finally, you can become an approval-seeking adult as a result of your school teachers. Even when they don't intentionally try to make you feel inferior, their daily actions can have a lasting impact on your sense of worth. Let's say your middle-school geography teacher always called on you in class, even though he knew that geography wasn't your strong point. You tried your best, but could never give the right answer. If your teacher never said anything to you, you always felt like he and your classmates were judging you. Once you graduate, you continue to fear to be stupid, even after you realize you can have a successful life without knowing the capital of

Alaska. You'll still feel the need to overcompensate by presenting yourself as a genius. Even if it means rambling on about a subject, you know nothing about or refusing to admit when you're wrong about something.

It's easy to turn to validation when we face all these pressures in our physical lives. It becomes even harder to turn away when we face constraints in our virtual lives. Social media platforms like Instagram, TikTok, Twitter, and Facebook have their benefits (Buckley, 2018; Hopper, 2019). They can be a great tool to connect with others, especially when physical distances separate you. But this instant connection comes at a price—namely, the need for immediate attention and validation.

As a social media user, your personal worth depends on how many likes, retweets, favorites, and comments you receive. To feel good about yourself, you try to maximize these rewards––not only from people you know but also from strangers. Yet, the more you live your life by trying to please your social media friends and followers, the less likely you'll be to do things to please yourself. Everything aspect of your life becomes an opportunity to be seen and praised. When you don't receive this praise, you feel worthless.

"By living our lives through social media, we become addicted to likes, favorites, retweets, and comments that validate our sense of worth (Woodall, 2018)."

No matter where validation comes from, it brainwashes you to behave in specific ways so you'll receive the positive responses that you crave (Geddis, 2018). The more you are praised when you do or say something, the more you will repeat those actions to bring out future praise. As a form of operant conditioning, validation reinforces these actions so that over time, it becomes instinctual to do or say things that win approval from others (Staddon & Cerutti, 2003). And once approval seeking is instinctual, you become a prisoner to this feedback loop (Buckey, 2018; Uniacke, 2018). You stop trusting yourself to make your own choices. You lose the ability to judge what is right and what is not. Worst of all, it makes people disapprove of you in the long run.

Most people can easily see through approval-seeking behavior. They can distinguish a real compliment from a fake compliment. They can tell when you're pretending to know more about a subject that you're clueless about. They may be interested in your juicy bits of gossip, but worry that you'll also say mean things about them behind their back. In short, they'll see you as fake, needy, and untrustworthy.

To be seen as genuine, self-assured, and reliable, you'll need to tell your approval-seeking behavior to fuck off. By replacing your validation with healthier ways to measure your worth and abilities, you'll regain the confidence you need to control your life.

HOW WE CAN OVERCOME IT

As I said in Chapter 3, one of the best ways to overcome your insecurities is to get in touch with your authentic self.

When you reconnect to your needs, wants, and desires, you'll feel more confident about who you are and what you're capable of. You'll realize that you are enough, just as you are, without needing to hear others confirm that for you.

Some other methods will squash your need for external praise. Stand firm in your decisions, use negative feedback as an excuse to do better, find happiness away from social media, connect to your reason for being, and stay true to yourself, no matter the consequences. It takes a lot of practice to internalize these habits. But the more you make a conscious effort, the more natural it will become to find validation within yourself.

Be Decisive

The most obvious way to get over validation is to break the cycle. Don't be hard on yourself (Buckley, 2018; Uniacke, 2018). But give yourself a gentle reminder that you are entitled to your own thoughts and opinions. You don't need anybody's permission to make decisions about your life. So what if others disapprove? At the end of the day, your opinion is the only one that matters.

The best place to start is with simple decisions that don't have enormous consequences. Let's say you're ordering Chinese takeout with your roommates. You're debating between chow mein or fried rice. Instead of asking your roommates, make a choice yourself. Maybe they will tell you that the fried rice is no good. Perhaps you'll decide on the rice anyway, take your first bite, and wish you'd listened to them. But at least you'll have the satisfaction of being in control of your dinner. Plus, you'll be more informed next time you want to order from the same restaurant.

Once you get more comfortable making small decisions for yourself, you can graduate to making more significant decisions. You may still look to others for the occasional bit of advice or inspiration, especially if they have knowledge that you don't have (Varshika G, 2019). For example, if you're considering moving to a new neighborhood, ask for your coworker's opinion if they already live in that neighborhood. Respectfully consider what they have to say. But at the end of the day, it's your decision whether or not to move.

Another critical aspect of being decisive is learning to say no (Buckley, 2018; Strauss Cohen, 2018). You'll save time, money, and energy by doing it. You'll also avoid endless to-do lists that weigh you down and prevent you from enjoying life to the fullest.

As you become more confident with making your own choices, you'll free yourself from the need for validation. You'll start living a life that brings you joy, even if people criticize you for it.

Adopt a Growth Mindset

Nobody likes being rejected or criticized for their actions or beliefs. In a perfect world, we'd get every job we apply for, date every person we had feelings for, and receive nothing but praise every time we tried something new. But we don't live in a perfect world. Whether we deserve it or not, rejection and criticism are an inescapable fact of life.

When you face negative feedback from others, you have two options. You can have a fixed mindset, where you see it as a personal failure (Uniacke, 2018). Or, you can have a growth mindset, where you see it as an opportunity to improve.

Remember that disapproval is not the same as hate (Varshika G, 2019). Frequently, it's the people who care the most who call you out if you're doing something wrong. This can range from the Parisian friend that corrects your French pronunciation to the muay thai instructor who critiques your roundhouse kicks. They don't do these things to be mean. They just want you to reach your full potential. Of course, there's a difference between correcting mistakes and constantly attacking someone, as seen in the critical mother example. In this case, they're just being critical for the sake of being critical. And this is a reflection of their own insecurities instead of your supposed incompetence. Remember that constructive criticism is built on good intentions, not malice.

Keeping this in mind, don't be afraid to give negative feedback as well as receive it (Buckley, 2018). If a restaurant gives you lousy service, write a review to discuss what they could have done better calmly. If an online store messes up your order, notify them of the mistake and send it back. You have the right to do these things. As long as you do it respectfully, there's no reason to feel bad about someone else's mistake. Plus, if the restaurant or store owners also have a growth mindset, they'll be glad of your honesty.

You'll receive similar benefits when you offer up your beliefs, as well as your abilities, to criticism. When you allow your social, political, and religious opinions to be challenged, you see problems from new perspectives and discover new solutions. You can develop new beliefs that better suit your needs and understanding. You can reinforce existing ones, after considering alternatives and deciding that yours is the most reasonable. It's a win-win situation, as long as you want it to be.

Nobody will ever agree with everything you say or think. That's one of the beauties of living in our world. We all have different opinions, and we can all learn from our differences. But don't be afraid to stick to what you believe, even if it seems like everyone else is against you. Even if they don't agree with you, people will respect you for staying true to yourself instead of copping out just to keep the peace.

By adopting a growth mindset, you can use the rejection and criticism of your actions and beliefs as an excuse to do better. This will give you the drive you need to reach your goals.

Focus on the Process

Part of having a growth mindset is recognizing that success is based on hard work. You can't expect to receive any reward without putting in the effort (Hopper, 2019;

Uniacke, 2018). This is why it's essential to focus on the journey itself, instead of just the destination. By doing so, you'll train your mind to live in your own moment instead of endlessly worrying about what others think.

Let's say you've signed up for a night class at your local business college. You could stress yourself out by constantly checking that your partner is okay with you being away from home on Wednesday nights. You could badger your friends for their opinions about whether or not you'll be able to pass the class despite your busy life. You could overcompensate for your insecurities by trying to wow your classmates in group discussions––even when you don't quite understand the case study you've just learned about.

Or, you could concentrate on the tasks in front of you right now. Focus on trying to understand lecture materials. Ask questions if you're unsure about something. Listen to others during class discussions. Think about what you can contribute once it's your turn to speak. Workaround your other daily commitments to schedule time to work on your assignments. Make Saturday night your night off, so you can spend time with your partner. Live in the moment and use your own judgment to tackle problems as they come up.

As you get used to focusing on the process, you'll be able to reach your goals faster and more effectively, without being weighed down by doubt. You'll find the value in learning and growing, without any clear reward at the end of it. Most importantly, you'll be so focused on your own path that you won't have time to look to your friends, family, coworkers, or social media followers to validate your choices.

Celebrate Your Life Offline

Once you get used to living in the moment, you'll be so busy living offline that you'll forget to talk about it online. You may lose a few followers in the process. But it'll be worth it to gain your peace of mind.

You don't have to delete your social media accounts, primarily if you rely on them to connect with long-distance friends and family. Still, it's a good idea to be mindful of what you share and how often you do it.

For example, it's normal to post important information and events, like when you survived the first day at a new job or found out the sex of your unborn baby. But what if you're always sharing unnecessary details about your life, like what you ate for lunch or how many pages you read of the new Stephen King book (Buckley 2018)? Or posting congratulatory messages for people who don't use social media, like writing a "Happy Birthday" message to your two-year-old niece?

Before you post anything, ask yourself if there's a reason behind it other than trying to get attention. If you can't think of any, stay offline. Enjoy your niçoise salad without snapping a picture. Push yourself to read another chapter instead of scrolling through your Twitter feed. Drive to your sister's house to wish your niece a happy birthday in person.

Remember that you can still feel good about something even if no one else knows about it.

Once you stop seeking recognition from other social media users, you'll realize that you don't need likes, favorites, comments, or retweets to feel good about your life (Hopper, 2019). You can find joy by celebrating the little things in life offline. And you'll only grow more confident in your ability to find your own happiness.

Find Your Ikigai

According to Strauss Cohen (2018), true happiness comes from doing what matters to you. It means finding success by discovering your individual passions and following your dreams. Hopper (2019) takes this idea even further by encouraging everyone to find their ikigai.

Ikigai is a Japanese word meaning "a reason for being." It gives us the purpose we need to get up in the morning, accomplish our daily activities, and pursue our personal goals.

A key aspect of ikigai is living in the moment. You become so caught up in the flow of life, that you stop thinking about what highlights to add to your Instagram story or what fun facts you can use to impress your colleague. As a result, you free yourself from the need to live up to others' expectations. Instead, you base your beliefs and actions around your inner joy.

"By connecting to your reason for being, you'll achieve the inner peace that allows you to take control of your life (Jeschke, 2018)."

In his article, Hopper (2019) includes a Venn diagram to illustrate this concept. It consists of four interconnected circles: "What You Love," "What You Are Good At," "What the World Needs," and "What You Can Be Paid For." At the intersections of two different circles, you find your passion (what you love and are good at), profession (what you are good at and can be paid for), vocation (what you can be paid for and what the world needs), or mission (what you love and what the world needs).

You can then combine two of these paths as a direction for your life. But each of these choices comes with their own difficulty. If you choose a profession that you're passionate about, you'll be satisfied with your job, but feel like you're useless in the grand scheme of the world. If you turn your vocation into a profession, you'll live comfortably but feel empty inside. If you make your vocation your mission, you'll live an exciting but uncertain life. If you follow a mission that you're passionate about, you'll be happy but struggle to make ends meet.

At the crossroads of all four circles, paths and directions are ikigai. It is the only option that satisfies all of our needs and desires while making a difference in the world. Once you find that balance, you can use your ikigai to find validation in your true self.

Don't Apologize for Being You.

You don't need anyone's approval to be yourself (Buckley, 2018). No matter what you do, you're never going to please everybody. Even if you don't have a conflict with others, you'll still have conflict within yourself when you suppress your values, beliefs, and dreams (Strauss Cohen, 2018). By being true to who you are, you'll find the happiness and confidence to follow your own path to success.

Maybe you were bullied in your younger days for knowing a lot about dinosaurs. But if paleontology is your ikigai, you don't need anyone's approval to make your dreams a reality. So don't apologize to your mother for not going to law school instead. Don't be sorry to your friends when you get excited about discovery and ramble on about its implications for how we understand the Triassic era. Don't apologize to your seminar professor when you forgot when exactly the Triassic era happened. Ditch your fears and worries. Replace them with an unshakeable belief in your intelligence, your work ethic, and your overall self-worth.

Still, having trouble finding your internal validation? Whenever you start to waver, Geddis (2018) suggests connecting to your "power place." Think of something that you're good at. It doesn't have to be anything significant. Focus on small accomplishments, like scoring free throws, growing house plants, or folding origami cranes. Think about how happy and accomplished you feel whenever you do this activity. Then channel that powerful feeling whenever you want to look for others for approval. Keep telling yourself that you've got this. It might take a while. But eventually, you'll start to believe it.

As Duval (2012) says, we're never completely immune to what happens in our external environment. But we can choose to find validation within ourselves instead of beating ourselves up when we don't receive it from others. This way, we'll set ourselves up for success instead of sabotaging our chance to find the happiness we deserve.

5

SELF-SABOTAGE

L ooking for others' approval isn't the only way we stop ourselves from reaching our goals. A lot of the time, we don't even look for outside opinions. We just decide for ourselves what we can't do or don't feel like doing.

Maybe you love others but hate yourself. Maybe you try to start good habits but always end up falling back in your old ways. Perhaps you dream big but never put in the effort to make your dreams come true. In all of these cases, you are using your insecurities to sabotage your chance of finding happiness (Ho, 2019).

Self-sabotage is a set of behaviors or thought patterns that prevent you from achieving your desired goals (Laderer, 2018; Raypole, 2019; Steph Social, 2020). This concept may seem strange at first. Why would someone purposely sabotage their own success? The truth is, nobody wants to fail. But, as we develop doubts and worries about our abilities, we pick up habits that prevent us from reaching our full potential. We may not even realize how destructive these habits are. This is what makes them so successful at getting in the way of our success.

Some common symptoms of self-sabotage include:

Blaming others: You refuse to acknowledge when your thoughts and actions keep you from reaching your goals. You're also overly critical of others and pick petty arguments just for the sake of arguing.

Giving up too quickly: Maybe you're lazy. Or maybe you have deeper issues, like fearing failure or criticism. Whatever it is, you put minimal effort into whatever you do. And when things get tough, you don't give yourself a chance to overcome your problems. You walk away.

Procrastination: You put things off when you don't feel like doing them. Maybe you're feeling overwhelmed and genuinely need a break. However, if you're always procrastinating, there's usually a more significant issue at play. For example, you could be afraid of taking on new responsibilities or dealing with possible negative consequences of your actions.

Being silent about your needs: To avoid conflict, you let people mistreat you. You resort to passive aggressiveness instead of being honest about your feelings. You also prefer to let others make decisions for you.

Self-criticism: You set high standards for yourself and become extremely hard on yourself when you don't meet them. You fill your mind with negative thoughts, believing that you're stupid, unloveable, or all-around unworthy.

Imposter syndrome: You feel like you aren't good enough to achieve the success that you've had. You're terrified that others will find out that you're a 'fake.'

Dating the wrong people: Instead of searching for romantic partners who are compatible with your needs and desires, you fall into relationships that are going nowhere. Maybe you're always dating the same type of person who disappoints you over and over again. Or maybe you stay with a partner even when you have conflicting life goals, hoping they'll someday change their minds.

Overindulging: When you're feeling down, you hide your emotions by overeating or abusing drugs or alcohol. You become addicted to that intense but temporary rush of good feelings whenever you eat a tub of ice cream or take a shot of whiskey.

Ultimately, these habits come from our need to protect ourselves from harm. As I mentioned in Chapter 4, safety is a basic psychological need. But self-sabotage isn't. It gets in the way of trying new things and going after your dreams

(Steph Social, 2020). If left untreated, it will continue to fuck up your life and stop you from achieving the happiness you deserve.

Let's get started by looking at the root causes of self-sabotage. Once you know where your bad habits come from, you can create a plan to achieve the confident, goal-driven life you've always wanted.

WHY WE HAVE IT

According to Ho (2019), self-sabotage is an evolutionary adaptation that has helped the human race survive. Before we decide on a course of action, we need to weigh the positive and negative outcomes. For example, before deciding to chase after a mammoth, early hunters had to determine whether it was better to attain the potential reward of a meal or avoid the potential threat of breaking a limb, being trampled, or being speared in the chase. Thankfully, most of us can avoid the threat of death or injury when we go to the grocery store for our food. But we still face similar dilemmas in our day-to-day lives, like deciding where to go to college or whether or not to ask out the cute barista at the neighborhood café.

"Success is all about achieving that balance between attaining rewards and avoiding threats (Mozhvilo, 2020)."

The problem is that rewards and threats are two sides of the same coin. Our brains release the same feel-good dopamine rush, whether we take a risk and attain rewards or stay safe and avoid threats. So, when we want to repeat similar behaviors to receive that same level of dopamine, we may not know which action to take. It's easy to throw our balance out of whack by focusing more on avoiding threats. When this drive is more potent than our drive to attain rewards, we become vulnerable to self-sabotage.

Ho (2019, n.p.) uses the acronym LIFE to identify the four root causes of self-sabotage: Low or shaky self-concept, Internalized beliefs, Fear of change or the unknown, and Excessive need for control. We usually develop these patterns in childhood, then carry them into our adult life.

Let's say you grew up with a step-father who was the glass-half-empty type. He always wanted to be an artist but ended up working as an accountant, claiming it was the more 'realistic' (read: safer) career choice. He tried to pass on this negative viewpoint to you by always pointing out potentially unpleasant or dangerous consequences to your actions. When you wanted to learn to ride a bike, he refused to take off your training wheels, insisting that you would crash without them. When you were excited about a gymnastics birthday party with your classmates, he told you the story about when his friend broke a leg doing cartwheels. When you took driving lessons with him, he gripped his armrests the entire time as he shouted at you to slow down on your turns. Your step-father probably only said these things because he wanted you to stay safe. But you might internalize his self-sabotaging perspective as a usual way of life.

You'll be more likely to avoid risks and play it safe. You'll shy away from trying new hobbies, and you'll give up on your dreams, doubting you could ever achieve them. You may even question your ability to accomplish everyday activities like driving a car or asking someone out.

Past relationship dynamics is another critical source of self-sabotaging behavior (Laderer, 2018; Raypole, 2019). Maybe you had a physically abusive partner. Or perhaps they were just selfish, always putting their needs ahead of your needs. If you don't recognize that your partner is at fault, you might think that this type of behavior is normal and/or deserved. Even after your relationship ends, your self-esteem might be so low that you are unable to stick up for yourself whenever someone treats you poorly or makes excessive demands on you.

Finally, self-sabotage can come from fear of failure or lack of control. Let's say that after a blissful few years, you've realized that your partner is a taker, never giving back their share of time and effort to make the relationship work. Feeling like a doormat, you break up with them and vow that you'll never get into that position again. As you start to date new people, you'll be extra cautious about how the relationship progresses. You'll bolt at the first sign of conflict, like when your partner asks you for big favors. You might even start to worry when things are going well, fearing that things are too good to be true. You might try to gain the upper hand by being the one who makes demands. Even as you pick fights and push your partner away, you think it's better for your relationship to end than open yourself up to feeling vulnerable again. But your unhealthy habits will only make you feel more insecure about relationships, sabotaging your chance of finding love.

The symptoms and sources of self-sabotage may seem more complicated than other forms of insecurity. But this doesn't make it any more challenging to overcome than comparison, worthlessness, or validation. The first step is to recognize where self-sabotage comes from, looking for common patterns in your thoughts or behaviors (Raypole, 2019; Steph Social, 2020). For example, if you're always procrastinating on essential projects, the self-doubt you received from your stepfather is preventing you from taking action. If you're always afraid of opening up to your friends, partners, or coworkers, your past relationship trauma is spilling out into other areas of your life.

Once you know your triggers, you'll be better equipped to define your self-sabotaging behaviors and find the right ways to overcome them.

HOW WE CAN OVERCOME IT

You can never progress if you insist on staying put (Steph Social, 2020). This applies to any insecurity that makes excessive demands on your wellbeing. Take responsibility for your own actions, be upfront about your wants and desires, push yourself to leave your comfort zone, and let go of negative influences that hold you back. The result? You'll be able to tell your self-sabotage to take a hike and start living the happy, confident life that you want to live.

Recognize the Problem and Take Accountability

Whenever you catch yourself sabotaging your chance of success, don't let it pass. Give yourself a firm but gentle talking to. Instead of blaming your behavior on external sources, identify the thought processes that make you act this way (Laderer, 2018; Raypole, 2019.

For example, if you're procrastinating on an important writing assignment, don't just say "I don't feel like writing" and retreat into a day of binge-watching Netflix and binge-eating chips. Think about the deeper reason behind your behavior. Are you worried that you won't do a good job? Are you stressed out from other life responsibilities? Once you've figured out why you're procrastinating, address the root causes of that issue and brainstorm ways to overcome it. Maybe you need to meditate and reaffirm your capability for success. Or, perhaps you need to ask your family for a weekend break from cooking and cleaning so you'll have more time to dedicate to the assignment. Whatever it is, you'll be able to take responsibility for your procrastination instead of distracting you from your work.

This applies to relationships too. Maybe you broke up with your partner for the valid reason that they were always possessive and jealous. But instead of laying all the blame on your partner, reflect on your own behavior in the relationship. Did you try to reach out to them to talk about their insecurities? Did you dismiss their concerns and say they were just 'crazy?' Did you contribute to their jealousy by constantly flirting with other people or blowing them off to spend time with your work colleagues? This doesn't excuse your partner's behavior. But by recognizing the consequences of your actions, you'll be able to take responsibility for your role in the breakup and find healthier relationships in the future.

It's also important to recognize and apologize to others when you take out your self-sabotaging frustrations on them. Did you pick an argument with your partner and intentionally hurt their feelings? Just because you had a moment where you doubted their affections for you? Apologize. Explain to them why you did this. It can be scary to open up about your negative feelings. But talking aloud about your issues will help ease the pain of your insecurities. And if your partner truly cares about you, they'll help you work on overcoming self-sabotage so you can make your relationship stronger.

Once you get comfortable viewing your self-sabotage patterns from an outside perspective, you'll be able to recognize the internal sources of your behavior instead of accepting it as a given or blaming it on external circumstances. You'll adopt healthier habits to overcome your doubts and fears and set yourself on a positive path to achieving your goals.

Declare Your Goals

Self-sabotage involves looking for a way out of a problem (Raypole, 2019). You don't want to fail, so you try to avoid it altogether. Yet, by avoiding the possible threat of failure, you're also avoiding the potential reward of success. So, instead of focusing on what you don't want to happen, focus on what you do want to happen. Declare your goals out loud. Then, follow the path to make them a reality.

I've said it before, and I'll repeat it––nobody is perfect. Everybody makes mistakes now and then (Laderer, 2018; Steph Social, 2020). But everybody also has the chance to succeed. And the first step to success is honest about your wants and desires.

Tell your family and friends about what you want to achieve. Voicing your goals out loud will make them seem more real to you. As you visualize them clearly in your mind, they'll look less like some foggy futuristic vision. Instead, you'll realize that they're a set of smaller tasks that you can work toward right now.

Focusing on big life goals can be daunting. So, to avoid the rise of self-doubt, break them into bite-sized tasks. Then, create a detailed plan to make it all happen. For example, if you want to run your own landscaping business, draw up a five-year plan with everything you want to accomplish. Be specific, giving yourself step-by-step instructions from purchasing your equipment to networking with potential customers and developing a weekly schedule to hire employees of your own. Give yourself specific time frames to get everything done. For example, you might want to start your business with a handful of lawns in the same neighborhood. The summer after that, you might want to add on five new lawns in an adjacent neighborhood. And so on and so forth.

You can also save yourself from self-sabotage by celebrating small achievements. Maybe you designed the perfect flyers to distribute in your neighborhood. Maybe you trimmed a hedge in record time. Perhaps you got your first recommendation from one of your customers. Every step you take is one step closer to achieving your dreams.

And if something doesn't work out? Put each problem in perspective. One bad review on your company's Facebook page doesn't make you a failure. Neither does getting rained out on a sod installation job. Remind yourself that you still deserve success. Then work even harder to earn those good reviews and plan your work around the weather forecast.

Once you get in the habit of declaring your goals and developing concrete plans to achieve them, you'll be able to push yourself out of your comfort zone. This way, you can start attaining rewards instead of just avoiding risks.

Get Out of Your Comfort Zone

When you self-sabotage, you stick to the limits that you set for yourself (Laderer, 2018; Steph Social, 2020). You stay in a job you hate because it's easier than starting your career from scratch. You stay with a friend group that takes advantage of you because it's easier than making an effort to look for new ones. You stay single because it's easier to rely on yourself than to risk having your heartbroken.

Overcoming your doubts and fears is never easy. It's very uncomfortable. You'll have many days when you'll feel like giving up and accepting your negative beliefs about yourself and your abilities. But you can never hope to gain big rewards unless you're willing to take significant risks.

"Success begins where your comfort zone ends (Lauton, 2016)."

The best way to start edging out of your comfort zone is to accept that your fears and frustrations are usual. Our negative emotions are essential tools that help us avoid potentially dangerous and unpleasant situations. But this doesn't mean they have to keep us from potentially rewarding situations either. That's why it's important to communicate about your feelings instead of running from them.

Let's say you had a fantastic date. Your feelings are growing stronger each day. But because of your past trauma, you're worried that the other person doesn't feel the same about you. Usually, when you feel this vulnerable, you'd just ghost them and hope you eventually forget about the person. Instead, be honest with your date. Ask them how they feel and what they're hoping to get out of the relationship. Then, share your own perspectives. Either you'll both have the same answers and be able to work out a situation that appeals to both your needs and desires. Or else you can end the relationship and look for someone who is a better match for you. It's a lot more challenging to have this conversation than to just run away and wonder later if you made the right decision. But the reward of true love is worth the risk of being rejected.

Once you get used to being honest about your romantic feelings, you'll find it much easier to deal with relationships that end prematurely or badly. You'll see it as an unpleasant but a manageable fact of life instead of a life-ruining judgment on your worth as a person. Better yet, you'll have a clearer idea of what kind of person you want to be with. You'll know how you can look for that person in the chaotic dating scene.

With the right mindset, you can turn your self-sabotaging behaviors on their heads and find the confidence to take risks to go after what you want.

Let Go

We often hold on to things that bring us a false sense of security because they feel comfortable and familiar (Laderer, 2018; Raypole, 2019; Steph Social, 2020). But to stop sabotaging your chances of finding happiness, you need to let go of everything that does not serve your purpose. This includes:

The past: Not everything that happened in the past is doomed to repeat itself. So, don't get weighed down by bad experiences. You can still remember them and learn from them. But don't let this stop you from imagining a better future yourself, where you achieve your goals and gain the confidence you deserve.

Toxic people: Whether it's friends, coworkers, partners, or even family members, there's always someone that wants you to fail. Cut these negative people out of your life and replace them with people who believe in you and encourage you to reach your goals. You'll thank yourself for doing this.

Control: Life is unpredictable. You cannot control everything that happens to you when you go out into the world. But you can control how you react to it. Ironically, the more you let go of things you can't control, the more you gain control of your own life. Instead of endlessly fighting against people and systems that cannot be dominated, you can focus on changing yourself. This way, you can work *with* instead of *against* your limitations to find success.

Negative thoughts about yourself: As our preschool teachers told us if you can't say anything nice about someone, don't say anything at all. This includes ourselves. Be kind and supportive of yourself, even when you make mistakes or relapse into old habits. Remember that as long as you're trying to be a better you, you're still worthy of success. You may not believe it at the start. But if you keep repeating your affirmations every day, you'll eventually exchange your fears and doubts for genuine self-confidence.

As you surround yourself with positive internal and external influences, you'll learn to stop being your own worst enemy and start being your own best friend (Laderer, 2018). And all of those self-sabotaging behaviors will stay in the past, clearing the way for a future free from unnecessary doubts and anxieties.

6

SOCIAL ANXIETY

At this point, you might be wondering what happens when you can't push yourself to leave your comfort zone. What if you want to love yourself, but you feel like everyone hates you? What if your body literally freezes whenever you have to give a presentation in front of your classmates or colleagues? What if you feel your tongue dry up and your words catch in your throat whenever you try to share your feelings? If this is true, then your insecurities go beyond the kind of self-sabotage that comes with procrastination or imposter syndrome.

Though it's often confused with shyness, social anxiety runs much deeper than this (Bridges to Recovery, 2018; Mayo Clinic, 2017; Rauch, 2017). Some people are naturally more reserved than others. And everyone experiences situations where they don't feel they're most confident. But not everyone develops an intense and irrational fear of specific social interactions. Usually, this happens in unfamiliar situations or ones where you will be watched by others.

In its most severe form, social anxiety morphs into social anxiety disorder (SAD), where you experience panic attacks or other disabling reactions that prevent you from enjoying life. Affecting over 15 million Americans, SAD is the second most commonly diagnosed anxiety disorder in the US, after specific phobias.

"Social anxiety involves a deep and irrational fear of social interactions. In its most severe form, it can lead to panic attacks (Fernando, 2018)."

Doctors and psychiatrists have identified many physical, emotional, and behavioral symptoms of social anxiety (Felman, 2018; Mayo Clinic, 2017; Smith et al. 2018). These include the following:

Physical symptoms: blushing, trembling, sweating, hyperventilating, fast heartbeat, muscle tension, numbness, dizziness, nausea, diarrhea, dry mouth, and throat.

Behavioral symptoms: avoiding eye contact, staying quiet to avoid attention, overanalyzing behavior in social situations, being self-critical, skipping school or work commitments, abusing alcohol, or drugs to calm the nerves.

Emotional symptoms: fear of interacting with strangers, being judged by others, being embarrassed or humiliated, accidentally offending someone, being the center of attention, appearing anxious to others.

Some socially anxious people experience all of these symptoms. Others only experience a handful. For example, people with performance social anxiety disorder may fear speaking or to perform in public, but feel at ease when having one-on-one conversations with strangers. Similarly, someone with mild social anxiety may feel uncomfortable with one-on-one interactions but speak comfortably during a presentation. It's all highly subjective.

What is common across the social anxiety spectrum is that there are certain social situations where you don't feel anxious (Bridges to Recovery, 2018; Mayo Clinic, 2017). This might include interacting with trusted friends and family, or speaking in public about a topic you're confident about. Still, because you experience anxiety in at least some situations, you risk lowering your quality of life. You may lose out on a career or academic advancement, avoid traveling to new places, fear criticism, lack assertiveness, abuse drugs, and alcohol, develop depression, and suffer from overall low self-esteem.

Social anxiety is a real pain in the ass. Even when it isn't as severe as SAD, it can still fuck up your life and make you think the worst about the world. But with a rational understanding of your triggers and a tailor-made plan to face them, you can grab a better hold on managing your anxiety.

WHY WE HAVE IT

Social anxiety is usually diagnosed in your teenage or early adult years, but symptoms typically start in childhood (Bridges to Recovery, 2018; Mayo Clinic, 2017; Rauch, 2017). Children who are shy, are teased for stutters or tremors, or have parents with social phobias are more likely to become socially anxious. You might inherit through your genes, your environment, or some combination of the two.

Some people are born with what's called a behaviorally induced temperament. This means that they withdraw from environments that they aren't familiar with, like social gatherings with strangers. Others are born with an insecure attachment style, which means that they're afraid of trying new things or interacting with strangers. Those with anxious-ambivalent insecure attachment experience this anxiety when a parent or other attachment figure does not accompany them. Those with anxious-avoidant insecure attachment experience anxiety whether or not their attachment figure is there. This is because they have trouble bonding with their parents or trusted adults. As a result, they lack the confidence to face their fears and achieve success.

Many socially anxious people also show an imbalance in their brain chemistry. They might have heightened automatic emotional processing or a deficiency in neurotransmitters like dopamine, serotonin, oxytocin, or glutamate. There's often a genetic basis for these deficiencies. For example, gene SLCGA4 controls serotonin, which helps you stabilize your mood and feel calm. Having too much or too little can lead to anxious feelings.

Other times we develop anxiety when specific structures in our brains aren't functioning properly. The amygdala is the part of the brain that's responsible for your "fight-or-flight" response. It's a valuable tool that helps you stay alive by pushing your bodily functions into overdrive whenever you're in danger. But if your amygdala is hyperactive, it will mistake non-threatening social situations for hazards. It will trigger anxiety symptoms, like muscle tension, high blood sugar, and hyperventilation. These surges also shift your brain's focus to the right prefrontal cortex. This area is supposed to calm the amygdala once it decides that there are no real threats. But when your prefrontal cortex is also out of whack, it will also allow your amygdala to react as if you're facing real, life-threatening danger.

Childhood and early adulthood are critical times for brain development. So, if we develop social anxiety during these years, it's easy for these habits to become ingrained in our brains (Mayo Clinic, 2017; Rauch, 2017). Let's say you had a parent in the military and moved to a different city every few years. Because you always had to start over at a new school with a new friend group, you always felt like an outsider, even if others seemed to accept you. Or maybe you spent your entire school years with the same group of people who bullied you for not wearing the right clothes or being a "teacher's pet." You tried to involve your teachers or the school principal, but nothing was ever done. You might have even confided in your parents, only to be told you were being silly or imagining things. Because of this, you'll keep your anxious feelings to yourself, even as they bubble up and prevent you from comfortably interacting with people.

You can also develop social anxiety at home if you have overprotective parents who keep you from doing 'dangerous' things. As an adult, your brain will be hyperactive and try to keep you from social situations that aren't dangerous, like speaking in public or networking at a business conference. Or you can develop it from excessive technological use. By limiting your face-to-face interactions with others, you never become comfortable interacting with them.

No matter where your social anxiety comes from, once you have it, you develop triggers that cause you to experience panic attacks or other symptoms (Bridges to Recovery, 2018; Cunic, 2020b; Felman, 2018; Mayo Clinic, 2017; Rauch, 2017). These triggers can include:

Performances: these range from athletic competitions to public speaking. Anything that positions you as the center of attention.

Meeting new people: this fear can happen at parties or other social gatherings where you only know one or two people—or no one at all.

Making small talk: talking about yourself, the weather, or your weekend plans makes you worry about sounding stupid or annoying. This feeling can be even stronger if you are talking to an authority figure, like an employer or teacher. Or if you are in a situation where you don't expect to make small talk, like standing in line at a grocery checkout or running into an acquaintance on the street.

Making eye contact: you don't want to feel vulnerable, so you focus your gaze anywhere else.

Being teased: you take it personally when others tease you, taking it as a sign that they don't like you.

Entering a room where everyone is seated: you feel like people are judging you when you're the last one to take a seat. Or you fear that your late arrival has caused a delay in the meeting, performance, speech, etc.

Dating: this is one of the most common triggers for social anxiety. It can include any aspect of dating life, from talking on the phone to going on physical dates to becoming physically intimate.

Writing and reading: you worry that your hands will shake while you're writing or that your voice may waver while you're speaking.

Stating your opinion: to avoid criticism, you keep your thoughts and beliefs to yourself. You may even pretend to agree with others when you don't.

Eating in front of others: you don't want to spill your food or have your hands shake while you drink. So, you eat all your meals in private.

Returning purchases to a store: you avoid calling attention to yourself by accepting what you've purchased, even if it doesn't work correctly.

Using public bathrooms: paruresis, also called shy bladder syndrome, makes you worry that others will judge you based on what they hear or smell.

Stress: Any form of physical or mental stress can aggravate social anxiety by increasing your heart rate, breathing rate, and blood sugar.

The more you experience these triggers, the more you'll fill your mind with negative thoughts about your worth and abilities. You might think that everyone hates you, that you have nothing to offer, or that you will choke, throw up, or faint once you try to speak.

When you start feeling anxious, it's tempting to try to control a situation by imagining bad things before they happen or putting yourself down before others can. But when you always doubt that social situations can be anything but painful and that people can be nothing but judgmental, you fail to see your reality for what it truly is. Like the self-sabotaging behaviors from Chapter 5, social anxiety keeps you from achieving your goals by filling your mind with irrational doubts and fears.

But once you know where your social anxiety comes from and what activities trigger it, you can learn to not only cope with these negative thoughts. You can also change them into positive thoughts that drive you toward success.

HOW WE CAN OVERCOME IT

Because SAD is a severe mental health disorder, you'll need to seek professional help to diagnose and receive treatment (Cuncic, 2020b; Felman, 2018; Mayo Clinic, 2017; Rauch, 2017). Depending on how badly it affects you, you might need anti-anxiety medication. Yet, in most cases of mild to moderate social anxiety, you can get by with behavior-focused strategies.

It's always best to talk to a psychologist before you try any anxiety-reducing techniques. But most professionals agree that the more you avoid social situations, the more anxious you become. That's why it's essential to take action sooner rather than later. Work with a cognitive behavior therapist to replace your anxious instincts with healthier reactions in social interactions. Combining this cognitive behavior therapy with relaxation and self-talk strategies. This way, you'll gain the self-confidence you need to socialize without a tremble in your voice or hands.

Cognitive Behavior Therapy

Cognitive Behavior Therapy (CBT) is the preferred method for combating social anxiety disorder (Bridges to Recovery,

2018; Felman, 2018). It reprograms the parts of your brain that react negatively in social situations. This way, you can start seeing them as non-threatening and maybe even enjoyable. If you're diagnosed with SAD, you might begin CBT in a treatment program at a hospital. In mild and moderate cases, you'll continue to live at home and just attend weekly or biweekly sessions with your therapist.

There are two main components to CBT. The first is a technique called reframing negative thought processes. Instead of viewing your insecurities as permanent conditions, you learn to see them as temporary, situation-based feelings. For example, rather than identifying as a "shy person," you reframe this by saying you "acted shy at the party last Saturday." This way, you start to see your social anxiety as a mindset that can be changed with the right tools. The second component is exposure therapy, where you gradually work up to facing triggering situations and learning to cope with them.

Let's break this down into a few key steps. First, your therapist will ask you to list the things that make you anxious (Leahy, 2014). It may help keep track by writing them down in a journal or recording them in an anxiety app like Worry Watch, Mindshift, or Pacifica (Cuncic, 2020b). Once you have your list, rank each item on a scale from 0 (not anxiety-inducing) to 10 (a panic attack) (Leahy, 2014). Your list might look something like this: dating (7), meeting new people (9), large crowds (7), running into people unexpectedly (8), eating in public (5). Add your worst-case predictions for each scenario. This might include being laughed at, being talked about behind your back, or panicking and saying something stupid.

Next, you'll be asked to identify your safety behaviors. This might include having a drink or smoke before your date, obsessively rehearsing what you're going to say before you meet someone new, scrolling through your phone when you're in a crowd of strangers, pretending to have dietary restrictions at a potluck, or avoiding eye contact when you pass people on the sidewalk. As you make this list, consider some problems associated with each behavior so that you can see their negative consequences. For example, you might have developed a cough from too much smoking or might be anxious about being away from your phone, even in your own house.

After you've sorted out your triggers and negative coping mechanisms, it's time to replace your anxious thoughts with rational thoughts. Imagine that you're in a triggering social situation, like a house party. Think about each action you would take at that party, from walking in the door to greeting the host to meeting their friends that you don't know. Identify each step that introduces a negative thought and consider how you could replace it with something more positive. For example, you might remind yourself that half the people in the room will be so involved in conversations that they won't even look up when entering the room. Or that the host probably wouldn't have invited you to the party if they didn't like you. Or that the people you meet will be more focused on thinking about what they're going to say than noticing that your palms are sweaty or that your heart is racing. As you focus on these thoughts, you'll feel your anxiety lower bit by bit.

Finally, you'll start your exposure therapy by putting yourself in social situations that make you anxious. Avoid your safety behaviors by showing up sober to your date, keeping your phone in your pocket at the party, and smiling at each person you pass on the sidewalk. Repeat you're positive, rational thoughts for yourself each step of avoiding triggering your social anxiety. If you're having trouble relaxing, you might even want to exaggerate your symptoms. For example, if you're worried about sweaty palms, don't dry your hands after washing them. If anyone asks about it, say you forgot. Or, if you say something you didn't mean to, make a joke of it. This will help you relax and better control your anxious feelings.

Once your social interaction is over, it's important not to overanalyze your actions. This will only trigger your anxiety. Instead, reward yourself for facing your fears and putting yourself out there. Make yourself a healthy treat that you enjoy. Watch an episode of your favorite show. Have a solo dance party to your favorite tunes. Whatever you like. You deserve it.

CBT may seem scary at first. But over time, these things will become second nature. You'll probably never become a social butterfly. Still, you'll at least be able to control your anxiety instead of having it control you. You'll develop healthier habits for interacting with people and feel more at ease than ever before.

Relaxation Strategies

When you have mild or moderate social anxiety, relaxation strategies can help you manage your symptoms. They can lower your heart rate and breathing rate, ease your muscle tension, and reduce your chance of a panic attack, especially when you combine them with CBT and a low caffeine diet (Brown, 2010).

One of the most popular relaxation strategies is diaphragmatic breathing (Cuncic, 2019a). This is a type of deep breathing that's used in yoga, meditation, and other mindful activities. When you try it for the first time, do it in a safe environment, like your home. Place one hand on your stomach and one on your chest. Inhale for three seconds, feeling your stomach balloon in front of you as it swells with air. Pause. Then exhale for three seconds, feeling your stomach retract toward your ribcage. Continue this inhalation-exhalation pattern for five to ten minutes.

Once diaphragmatic breathing comes naturally to you, you'll be able to use it whenever you start to feel anxious. Take a few deep breaths, focusing on the rhythm of your stomach as you inhale and exhale. You'd be surprised how quickly this can clear your mind and help you relax.

Progressive muscle relaxation (PMR) is another technique that's been around since the 1930s (Cuncic, 2019b). It was initially designed to help people sleep better. Yet, it's also been proven to help treat mild anxiety.

Once again, find a quiet place free from distractions. Wear loose clothes and remove your glasses or contacts. Take diaphragmatic breaths as you close your eyes. As you breathe, slowly move down your body, squeezing your muscles for 15 seconds. As you slowly release them for 30 seconds, you'll feel your tension disappear. Start with the forehead, then the jaw, then the neck, shoulders, arms, hands, buttocks, legs, and finally the feet. You may want to use an audio recording from YouTube or Spotify to help guide you during this exercise. Over time, the tensing and releasing patterns will become so ingrained in your muscle memory that you'll do it without thinking. And you'll find it much easier to face your daily challenges with a calm mindset.

Finally, guided imagery visualization can help you relax by inviting you to connect with an imaginary place that brings you comfort (Cuncic, 2020a). Many people like to picture a sunny beach with rolling ocean waves. Others prefer a warm, crackling campfire. You can pick whatever works for you, as long as you can imagine it vividly. You might even start with an audio track for inspiration.

"Guided imagery visualization involves drawing on your five senses to imagine a calming scene (Y-C, 2019)."

Like PMR, begin your visualization in a quiet place while wearing loose clothing as you close your eyes and fall into the rhythm of your diaphragmatic breathing, transport yourself to your place. Draw on your five senses to make it come to life. For example, you might imagine that you're bundled up in a warm fleece blanket, watching the flames from your campfire leap up to the starry sky. You watch a piece of timber fall into the embers, emitting tiny red sparks as it crackles. The pleasant smell of woodsmoke wraps around you like the blanket that you pull tighter around your shoulders. Continue to add this visualization for as long as you like. Then slowly count backward from 10 and open your eyes. You'll feel much more relaxed for the rest of the day.

There are also some personal relaxation strategies that you can do at home before you go out to socialize (Felman, 2018). You can play video games, draw, listen to your favorite album, do some stretching or anything else that you find enjoyable. If you leave the house feeling happy and relaxed, you'll be better equipped to deal with your anxious feelings whenever you meet new people at the house party or deliver that important presentation. Instead of allowing them to derail you, you can shake them off and replace them with positive self-talk.

Self-Talk Strategies

If your social anxiety has environmental rather than genetic causes, self-talk strategies are an effective way to help you cope with your symptoms (Cuncic, 2020b; Rauch, 2017);

Smith et al., 2018). Often, they're as simple as calling your-self out whenever you start to think negatively about your-self or others. These unhelpful thoughts include mind-reading (assuming you know others' thoughts), fortune-telling (predicting what will happen in the future), catastro-phizing (assuming that everything will go wrong), and personalizing (considering that everything is about you).

Let's say you're about to give a presentation at work. Feeling nervous, you tell yourself, "My coworkers will think I'm boring." Don't let this critical prediction slide. Ask yourself if you know for sure that they will think about this. Unless you've miraculously inherited psychic abilities, you're just making a blind assumption about what other people will think about you. Remind yourself of the times your coworkers have taken an interest in your work, like asking for your input on a project or praising you for the last slide show you put together. And if your coworkers don't show enthusiasm? Think of some other reasons why this might be the case. Maybe the office coffee machine stopped working, and everyone's suffering from caffeine withdrawal. Perhaps it's a Friday afternoon, and they're focused on their plans for the weekend. Maybe it's a Monday morning, and they're still hungover from the weekend. Whatever it is, it may not have anything to do with you. So, take a deep breath and tell yourself that you've got this. Bringing yourself up will help you feel less anxious. And you'll be more likely to deliver a confident presentation that wins a big round of applause from your coworkers.

Another aspect of positive self-talk is recognizing that you will make mistakes sometimes (Cuncic, 2020b). Maybe you identified all your triggers and safety behaviors in CBT but still snuck away for a smoke in the middle of your dinner date. Perhaps you practiced your diaphragmatic breathing and filled your mind with good thoughts, but your presentation still flopped. This doesn't make you a worthless mess. It just means that you need some more practice.

In the meantime, don't be afraid to make some adjustments and ask for help as you work on your social anxiety. Ask your confident friends if they have any tips to avoid the pre-date jitters. Stand behind a podium, desk, or something else you can hold onto so you have something to steady your shaky hands while you give your presentation. Take a break from the party to practice some PMR or guided visual imagery in a quiet place.

Once you feel more comfortable with your modified exposure tactics, you'll be more prepared to move onto more significant challenges and overcome them. Soon, you'll be replacing your irrational fears with positive thoughts about your worth and abilities. And your social anxiety will become just another insecurity that you can easily manage without allowing it to destroy your self-confidence.

7

(HUMBLE) BRAGGING

Of course, there is the danger of presenting yourself as too self-confident. Don't get me wrong—it's essential to feel good about yourself. But real confidence is believing in your personal qualities and abilities without feeling the need to brag about them. Otherwise, you're overcompensating for your insecurities instead of valuing who you really are.

Penguiny (n.d.) defines bragging as "personally imposing what-you-believe-to-be status-elevating thoughts on your audience" ("II What is Bragging?"). It happens when you go out of your way to remind others of what you think makes you worthy of praise. Overall, it has an "emotionally flattening" effect because the goal is to make yourself superior to others (AIPC, 2019).

According to the experts, there are six types of unacceptable bragging (Krauss Whitbourne, 2012; Penguiny, n.d.). This includes:

Directly drawing attention to your own great personal qualities: this is the most obvious form. You leave nothing to the imagination by telling people that you are smart, beautiful, talented, or rich. Full stop.

Directly drawing attention to something you've done: maybe you don't want to say that you're rich, smart, or talented, but you still want everyone to think it. So, you draw attention to yourself by doing or mentioning amazing feats. You might complain about spending $900 at a high-end store where you only bought three shirts. You might try to one-up somebody who talks about their Ph. D. studies at Stanford by saying you did your Ph. D. at Yale. Or, you might suddenly break out into an aria from *La Traviata*, even if no one asked for a demo of your opera skills.

Indirectly drawing attention to your own great personal qualities: this happens when you avoid praising your own attributes by quoting someone else's praise. This way, you seem to appear more modest. For example, you might say that your grandmother thinks you're beautiful or handsome, or that your professor claimed you wrote the best paper in your literature class.

Indirectly drawing attention to something you've done: maybe you posted a public thank you to organizers of a conference, but only so others would see that you attended.

Perhaps you posted a picture with your Porsche so that others would see how much disposable income you have. Or maybe you trapped someone into a conversation about skincare to bring up your 30-minute routine of cleansing and moisturizing. Whatever it is, you invite people to see how smart, rich, or beautiful you are through actions that subtly reference your good qualities.

Draw attention to your success with a 'disclaimer:' you might think it's better to brag if you let others know you're immodest. Yet, a brag is still a brag, even if you say "Not to toot my own horn, but I'm a great cook" or "I'm a great cook if I do say so myself."

Basking in someone else's glory: you attempt to make yourself great by associating with someone else whose qualities or achievements you're praising. For example, you might tell everyone at your new job that an intern you once mentored is now running their own company. Even though you're focusing on their accomplishment, you're only doing it to make yourself look smart and talented.

Another common form of bragging is 'humblebrag' (Krauss Whitbourne, 2018; Plata, 2018). This involves disguising a brag in the form of a complaint or anything else that makes you seem more humble, or at least more factual, about your greatness. Let's say you're an archaeologist who met the world's leading expert in Iron Age warfare at a conference. You might try to impress your colleagues by saying, "I'm so grateful I had the chance to meet him. I really wouldn't be where I am today in my career without his seminal research." You seem like you're modest, but you're just trying to name-drop. When you humblebrag, you recognize that overt bragging is socially unacceptable. But you hope that you can still get others to know your worth without looking down on you for being too proud.

In an appropriate amount, pride is essential for your self-esteem (AIPC, 2019; Barucija, 2019; Krauss Whitbourne, 2018; Penguiny, n.d.). It allows you to validate your self-worth and celebrate your hard-earned accomplishments. It's also not a crime, to tell the truth about your rewards or your elevated status if someone or something asks for it. You can proudly list your LinkedIn profile achievements or say that you live in an affluent neighborhood when someone asks where you live. This doesn't make you conceited.

What makes bragging different is that its exaggerated pride. It's a form of lying that makes you pretend to be Superman to feel good about yourself, even though you're secretly insecure about your powers. It encourages you to mislead others by only drawing attention to certain aspects of your life so that you can earn envy or sympathy.

The good news is that bragging or humblebragging is no different from any other type of insecurity. Once you know the reason behind it, you can cut the crap and start feeling appropriately confident about your worth and abilities. This way, you'll start earning proper compliments and praise—even if it's only coming from yourself.

WHY WE HAVE IT

There's been a lot of cognitive research on bragging in the past several years (AIPC, 2019). Perhaps the most exciting is a recent study at Harvard, where researchers took fMRI (functional magnetic resonance imagery) brain scans of people while they were sharing information about themselves. What they found that the areas that light up in the brain while we brag are the same areas that are associated with the pleasure we get from eating food or having sex. This neurochemical reaction explains why bragging can be so addictive. It's built into our brain chemistry!

Why do people start bragging in the first place? It all has to do with an inferiority complex (AIPC, 2019; Ghose, 2015; Krauss Whitbourne, 2015). When you feel lousy about yourself, you go about your days overcompensating through what's called "striving for superiority." You think that the only way you can feel happy is by making others unhappy. You may do this by showcasing either your achievements or the achievements of your friends and family members. For example, you might be retired now and feel like you don't have a lot of exciting things going on in your life. But if you have a granddaughter that's won trophies for her field hockey team, you might use her as an excuse to brag to your grandchildless friends to earn their praise and envy. This behavior may also reflect your fear of abandonment. You use your granddaughter's success in an effort to seem closer to her, even as she's growing up and spending more time with her friends than her family.

Braggarts also like to hide their insecurities by complaining that things aren't good enough for them. In a sense, bragging and complaining are flip sides of the same coin. They both monopolize conversations and make it all about you, even if you have to belittle others in the process. For example, you might have recently become wealthy and don't quite know how you're supposed to act in your new social position. To avoid being judged by "old money," you might criticize the food, the service, and the cleanliness of every event you attend, even when others look uncomfortable and try to change the subject. By doing so, you seem like a person with superior taste, despite your humble beginnings.

Narcissists are especially at high risk for bragging. Grandiose or overt narcissists have a tremendous sense of entitlement. Their inflated perceptions of their worth and abilities invite them to share these feelings with others constantly. Vulnerable or covert narcissists are a bit different. While grandiose narcissists may not realize that their behavior is based on hardwired insecurity, vulnerable narcissists are all too aware of this fact. Behind their cocky facade, they feel weak and helpless. So, they try to overcompensate for their negative thoughts by making others feel bad about themselves.

Like regular bragging, humblebragging is a product of shame (Plata, 2018). But this shame tends to be more external than internal. Despite all our talk about self-sufficiency and self-love, our Western society teaches us to hide our successes, so we don't exaggerate our worth. Narcissists ignore these social sanctions. But other insecure people try to get the best of both worlds, by combining their bragging with a touch of humility. They mistakenly believe that this will bring them the respect and admiration they crave.

These days, social media is a crucial arena for seeking praise (AIPC, 2019; Penguiny, n.d.). After all, platforms like Instagram and LinkedIn were explicitly invented for widespread self-promotion. To feel good about yourself, you may post or tweet about every single one of your accomplishments, whether it's something significant like buying your first house or something small like buying a new pair of shoes. Career websites also feed into this endless need to self-promote by telling us that this is how we show employers our value to receive job offers, promotions, and expensive retirement gifts. As a result, we become even more boastful, even when it works against us by alienating us from important people in our personal and professional lives.

"Social media platforms like Instagram encourage us to self-promote by bragging (Beliaikin, 2018)."

One of the core issues with bragging and humblebragging is that it creates an empathy gap (AIPC, 2019). The more you focus on yourself, the less you can connect with others and see things from their perspectives. You become trapped in a bubble that prevents you from improving your skills through constructive criticism or developing meaningful relationships with other people. It creates a lack of social awareness and instills you with a false sense of confidence that can devastate your self-esteem once the illusion is broken (Ghose, 2015).

For example, let's say you inherited your bragging behavior from your family. Maybe you had a grandmother who constantly bragged about your field hockey skills, even when you barely made it. She also hung your badly-drawn crayon art on the refrigerator, claiming that you would put Picasso to shame. She didn't just make you feel good about yourself––she made you feel better than everyone else. As a result, you grew up with an exaggerated sense of your own abilities. You thought that everyone would think as highly of you as your grandmother. But you'll be in for a rude awakening once you lose an important game or receive a bad grade in art class. As an adult, you'll be more likely to turn to brag about recapturing some of the praise your grandmother gave you, even though you secretly feel small and unsure of yourself.

Sometimes, bragging can be useful, like when it closes the gap in unequal relationships (Penguiny, n.d.). Let's say you're a working-class Londoner who lives in the Whitechapel area, and you meet the Duke of Marlborough. While he honestly introduces himself with his high-status title, you might invent a self-deprecating title for yourself, like the Vassal of Whitechapel. With this tongue-in-cheek brag, you might even make the Duke of Marlborough feel more at ease with you and less conscious of your social gap.

But for the most part, studies show that bragging makes people think less of your worth and accomplishments (AIPC, 2019; Ghose, 2015; Krauss Whitbourne, 2012; Krauss Whitbourne, 2018; Plata, 2018). We live in a culture that values modesty and demands hard proof before we believe what anyone tells us. Yet, many people are oblivious to these social norms. When they brag, they overestimate positive reactions and underestimate adverse reactions. They think it will earn them praise or admiration when it really makes them mistrust and dislike.

Even when you're humblebragging, people will see right through the disguise. Studies show that people think worse of complaint-based humblebrags than any other type of brag. After all, it relies on confusing mixed messages to try to make others feel bad about themselves. So, by humble-bragging, you become even more annoying, needy, and insecure than you would if you were just honest about your need to show off.

HOW WE CAN OVERCOME IT

The good news is that bragging doesn't have to be a permanent condition. We can find other ways to highlight those pleasure areas in our brains without exaggerating our worth and making others feel bad. In the case of narcissism, it might be challenging to overcome this hardwired way of thinking (AIPC, 2019). But if you learned to brag from your social media usage or your interactions with your family and peer group, you can unlearn it by changing the way you think and talk about yourself.

Once you learn to share your accomplishments by being thankful, honest, and humble, you'll be able to avoid triggering insecure behaviors in yourself and others. You'll also find the value in celebrating achievements for your own sake, without needing to impress anyone else.

Practice Gratitude

The best way to share your accomplishments without bragging is to emphasize how grateful you are (WikiHow, 2020). Focus on the process, not just the reward. And give credit to anyone who helped you along the way.

For example, instead of telling your colleague, "I'm so lucky I did my Ph.D. at Yale," say something like, "I'm so lucky Yale accepted my application. I learned so much from my supervisor. She really pushed me to deliver my best work." By doing this, you'll draw more attention to the hard work you put into your Ivy League degree, rather than just the degree itself. Instead of dismissing you as a snob, your colleague will recognize that you have a good reason to be a proud Yale alum.

And if they congratulate you? Just say thank you (Kwak, 2014). You don't need to downplay your success when others recognize it. As long as you maintain a balance between giving and receiving praise where praise is due, you'll feel comfortable about your qualities and abilities without ever needing to exaggerate them.

Correct Yourself

Sometimes we don't realize that we're bragging when we're just trying to share something about ourselves (Penguiny, n.d.). Especially when you're talking to someone you don't know, it's easy to draw on your own experience when you have nothing else to say. But be wary of talking about yourself too much. It can easily lead you to some form of bragging.

Whenever you catch yourself bragging to someone, stop what you're doing and apologize (AIPC, 2019). They'll appreciate the fact that you're trying to do better, even if the odd brag slips out now and again. If this feels too awkward, change the subject, so you're not tempted to continue showing off. An excellent way to do this is to ask the other person about themself. By asking others questions about their interests and accomplishments, you'll build better relationships and avoid the pitfalls of thinking too highly of yourself.

You can also correct your behavior by adopting healthier ways to self-promote. Recognize that social media is just a glorified snapshot of our lives instead of a true reflection of it (Barucija, 2019). Behind those photoshopped pictures and shiny list of achievements is someone who faces their own personal struggles, just like you. Breaking this illusion of perfection will help you stop competing with others and trying to out-brag them with likes, comments, or retweets.

If you want a better way to correct your bragging in the workplace, you can control it through a 'bragologue' (Kwak, 2014). This is a short story where you engage others with your accomplishments instead of just firing them off in a list. Focus on the facts and weave them together with great references to projects, awards, or other relevant experience. This way, you'll be able to show your potential or current employers that you've earned your success, instead of resorting to quick boasts that they may not believe.

As long as you present yourself honestly and humbly, there's no reason why you should have to shy away from self-promotion. Just like in your conversations, don't be afraid to correct yourself if you start to brag. Find a way around it and do better next time.

Be Humble

Whether you've been working for years to get promoted or to earn enough money to treat yourself to your dream car, it's normal to want to share the good news with others. But there are ways to do this while still staying humble.

Studies show that the most successful people are the ones who are open about their limitations (Barucija, 2019). They recognize that they still have a lot to learn and a lot of growing to do. They view success as a constant effort rather than something you earn once and maintain for life. So, whenever you start falling into the trap of exaggerating your accomplishments, remind yourself that you always have room for improvement. Once you get in the habit of doing this, it will become more natural to deflate your ego and concentrate on bettering yourself instead of earning praise.

Of course, this doesn't mean that you should never be honest about your accomplishments (Ghose, 2015; Douglas, 2019). It's okay to quote others who've given you praise at times when you need to convince others of your skills. But you should be prepared to back it up, so it's not just empty words. For example, if you're applying for a new job at an architecture firm, don't tell the office manager that you were the best architect at your last firm. Show him your portfolio. Bring him client testimonials. Mention any awards that you've won. Draw on your references from trusted sources to show that you're the best person for the job. Bragging is much more plausible when it's someone or something else that does it for you (Krauss Whitbourne, 2012). This way, you'll be able to assert your skills without resorting to bragging.

Being humble also means focusing less on yourself and more on others (Ghose, 2015; wikiHow, 2020). It means being kind by bringing people up instead of putting them down. It means recognizing that you don't have to compare yourself to anyone else to feel proud of who you are.

Let's say both you and your friend own sports cars. Your friend likes to brag about their vehicle, even though yours is newer and has more exclusive features. You could put your friend down by saying your car is better. Or, you could bring both of you up by saying that you both have nice cars. You'll make your accomplishments even more visible when you use your power to bring others up alongside you instead of tearing them down.

You may even set a positive example for others when you do this. By seeing how you still receive praise even when you're sharing the spotlight, your friend might stop their own bragging and follow your lead. Instead of trying to make yourselves superior to each other, you'll be able to support each other by recognizing your equal worth.

Avoid Sensitive Subjects

The problem with bragging and humblebragging isn't just that it's a reflection of our poor self-esteem––it affects others' self-esteem as well (Plata, 2018; wikiHow, 2020). It triggers their insecurities or personal struggles just so we can boost our egos.

Let's say you write a Facebook post in support of trans rights by saying, "As a cisgender person, I've never had to anyone try to silence me for being true to who I am." You may be attempting to show solidarity. But you're essentially patting yourself on the back for having the privilege to be you. Your trans friends who look at your post will see that you're using their discrimination to brag about yourself.

The best way to stop this is to be conscious of others' emotional triggers. You can still speak up about social justice issues without drawing attention to how considerate or 'woke' you are. Focus on the issue, not your reaction to it. Empathize with others and see where you can lend your voice to create actual change.

"Want to avoid bragging? Avoid sensitive subjects, like money (McCutcheon, 2018)."

Another way to avoid triggering others is to be conscious of topics that might hit a nerve. For example, avoid talking about money if you can. It's a constant source of stress for people on every step of the income ladder. Plus, it's nobody's business how much you make. Even if you're on the Sunshine List, people can look you up if they're curious. You don't need to share this information. And if you do have to talk about your salary, be as vague as possible. Saying "I earn a lot" will sound less like unnecessary bragging than "I earn $987,00 per year after tax."

Again, it's alright to be honest if people ask you for specifics about your achievements. But when offering up the information yourself, try to be as sensitive as possible. Keep a neutral tone, and stay humble. And remember that you don't have to share everything about yourself. You can still feel proud of yourself, even when no one else knows about it.

Brag to Yourself, Not Others

It's not only okay but also healthy to brag about your accomplishments to yourself (Krauss Whitbourne, 2012). Recognizing and validating your self-worth is vital for building a positive self-image and maintaining your confidence. It's also a great way to unleash your need to brag without annoying others in the process.

Kwak (2014) suggests keeping a journal where you record your accomplishments. Take note of what you learned, who helped you along the way, and what you can do better next time. This can apply to anything in your personal or professional life. Similarly, when it comes to your career, Douglas (2019) suggests keeping a private brag file of the work you're proud of and enjoyed doing. Taking stock of your achievements will help you take pride in your success without basing them off your feelings of shame or your need to compete with others. Instead, it will just be an honest belief in your worth and abilities.

There's a fine line between confidence and cockiness. But once you find that happy medium, you'll be able to boost your self-esteem and genuinely share your accomplishments. You won't have to overthink it by worrying that others will dislike you for believing in yourself.

8

OVERTHINKING

Y ou want to have genuine self-confidence. But what if it's not bragging that's holding you back? What if you're so busy worrying what other people think about you that you couldn't be a show-off even if you tried?

While it's good that you're keeping your ego in check, this doesn't mean that overthinking is any less dangerous to your self-esteem. Like any other insecurity, it holds you back from reaching your full potential. It fills your head with irrational fears and doubts and prevents you from enjoying life to the fullest.

Overthinking happens when you continuously analyze and agonize over your thoughts (Clark & Lehmann, 2019; Hakki, 2018; Hurst, 2017; Guerra, 2018; Mckibben, 2015; Morin, 2016; Schuster, 2018). It often involves rumination, where you mentally rehash past mistakes, become paralyzed by present decisions, and worry about future catastrophes. It turns even the most simple choices, like what to order for lunch, into a high-stakes situation. It can also become a meta-problem, where you overthink the fact that you're overthinking.

Because overthinkers become so wrapped up in their own thoughts, it's difficult for them to recognize their insecure behaviors. But you can usually tell when you're an over-thinker if you:

Buy into your false assumptions: you spend too much time in your head. Because of this. Your imagination runs wild. You always jump to the worst conclusions. You see everything in black and white.

Feel anxious about everything: you over-explain yourself to make sure people understand you. You put off appointments and plans because you're afraid something wrong will happen. You predict catastrophic events for your future and play these mental images on repeat until you give yourself a headache.

Lose focus: you space out because you get lost in your thoughts, even when others are speaking.

Look for meaning in everything: as a little kid, you're obsessed with 'why' questions. You always need to know why something happens and what you can do about it.

Take others' words too seriously: you analyze every word that someone tells you and are hypersensitive to what people think of you. You don't trust yourself to make your own judgments, so you let others make them for you.

Find it hard to let go: you put your heart into everything you do. And when something goes wrong, you feel like the universe is against you. You close yourself off from the world whenever your heart is broken or when your hard work ends in failure. You always worry about what you could have done better.

Obsess over getting everything right: you are a perfectionist. You continuously criticize yourself whenever you do anything wrong. You take forever to answer questions because you want to get the words right. Or you might not even answer at all. You work slowly so you can take care of every single detail. You put off challenges until you're ready to face them--if you're ever ready at all.

Try to mind read: you assume you know what others are thinking and believe it's always negative. You also assume everyone can read your mind without having to explain your thoughts out loud.

Over-plan: you don't want any nasty surprises. So, you need to figure out plans days or even months in advance. You're obsessed with lists--they help you plan everything in detail so that you won't forget anything.

Ask for reassurance: maybe you ask questions repeatedly because you want to make sure the answer is still the same. Or perhaps it's because you want to work out every possible outcome. You're not trying to be annoying. Your mind is just telling you something different every minute.

Apologize for no reason: you don't want anyone to think anything negative of you. Even the slightest change in someone's tone can set you off. As a result, you obsessively apologize so people won't be angry with you.

Struggle with decision making: you can't make split-second decisions without agonizing whether you made the right choice. You constantly weigh the pros and cons and think of every possible course of action. You paralyze yourself with your inability to act.

Overanalyze social interactions: you take note of every word in a conversation, every gesture, every tone change, every facial expression. After these interactions, you assess your performance and point out everything you did wrong. You exhaust yourself with worrying about whether you'll bore, offend, or anger anyone.

Did you think you were the only person who felt these things? Don't worry; you're far from alone. A recent University of Michigan study found that 73% of 25-35-year-olds and 52% of 45-55-year-olds are guilty of overthinking at least some of the time (cited in Ries, 2019). And in the UK, it's one of the leading causes of mental health issues (Psych-Alive, 2015).

Even confident people analyze their past actions and take the time they need to complete tasks (Guerra, 2018; PsychAlive, 2015; Ries 2019). This is normal. Introspection leads to greater self-understanding, which helps you reach your goals. But rumination is introspection gone wrong. It may seem like you're doing yourself a favor by worrying about real or imagined problems. But worrying about a problem makes you feel worse than the problem itself. It stresses you out for no reason, which means you're more likely to make the wrong decisions after all. It also fills your mind with destructive self-talk, keeping you from reaching your goals, and enjoying your life.

So, what can you do about it? How can you tell your over-thinking to fuck off once and for all? First, you'll need to dig deep to find out where this insecurity comes from. Spoiler alert: it all has to do with your brain chemistry.

WHY WE HAVE IT

Overthinking comes from the same part of the brain that's associated with fear and anxiety (Guerra, 2018; Hakki, 2018; Morin, 2016). So, if you already have an anxiety disorder, you're more prone to overthinking. And the more you over-think, the more you risk developing stress, anxiety, and depression. It's all a part of the same cycle.

"Anxiety disorders can lead to overthinking, and over-thinking can lead to anxiety disorders (Erfurt, 2018)."

You can also develop overthinking from other aspects of your personality. You may already be a perfectionist who pushes yourself to meet unrealistic expectations. Or maybe you're just a natural-born problem solver (Hurst, 2017). There's nothing wrong with having an analytical mind, as long as it doesn't get hung up on unproductive thoughts. In this case, it is more difficult for you to find the right solutions to your problems.

Like other insecurities, we often pick up overthinking from our childhood experiences (PsychAlive, 2015). Let's say you grew up with a step-mother who told you that you were no good. She always compared you to her biological children, asking why you weren't a genius like your step-sister or a natural-born musician like your step-brother. If you believe what your step-mother says, you'll grow up with a strong 'anti-self.' This is the part of you that criticizes your worth, doubts your abilities, and causes you to ruminate on your mistakes. It's the opposite of your real self, which is the part that validates your worth, celebrates your abilities, and sees mistakes as valuable learning opportunities. By always listening to your anti-self, you'll second guess how romantic partners feel about you, agonize over what to wear to a party, avoid strangers at the party in case you say something stupid, doubt if a weird bump on your skin merits a doctor's appointment, and worry you'll be fired for not laughing at your boss's bad jokes.

No matter where it comes from, overthinking has a devastating effect on your self-esteem (Guerra, 2018; Hakki, 2018;

Ries, 2019). It alienates you from the reality of your world, imprisoning you in negative thoughts. These thoughts soon wreak havoc on other parts of your life, causing:

Inaction: you never want to fail, so you stop trying. Like self-sabotage, it reduces your drive to succeed because you're so worried about possible threats.

Lack of creativity: overthinking can sometimes lead to fresh new ideas. But most of the time, it just creates a mental block. This makes it challenging to expand your mind beyond your existing thoughts and assumptions.

Stress: whenever your mind is in distress, these negative sensations are transferred to the rest of your body, thanks to a stress hormone called cortisol. Your heart rate increases, your breathing accelerates, and you may have a panic attack.

Lack of energy: too much cortisol in your system leads to burnout. Because you spend so much time with your thoughts, it's easy for you to become mentally exhausted.

Insomnia: when your breathing and heart rates are high, and your thoughts are racing, you can't relax enough to fall asleep. And when you don't get enough sleep, this just lowers your energy even more.

Low mood: when you always ruminate on your thoughts, it's easy to get stuck in a worry spiral. You eventually forget why you started thinking about a problem in the first place. But the millions of thoughts that the problem initiated leave you feeling anxious and out of control.

Change in appetite: cortisol increases your appetite, while other stress factors make you nauseous. As a result, you might turn to overeat or undereating.

When you're an overthinker, it's tempting to focus on the positives. It does bring certain strengths, like thinking critically, looking beyond the surface of complex issues, and taking care of every detail when completing a project (McKibben, 2015). After all, some of the world's greatest inventors and world leaders were overthinkers.

But when your constant ruminating over problems is causing you to lose sleep or become physically sick, these are signs that you're overthinking. It means that it's time to start addressing the real problem: your negative thought patterns.

HOW WE CAN OVERCOME IT

Once you recognize these unhelpful behaviors, the next step is to change how you think about yourself and the world around you. Overthinking may be a hard habit to break (Hurst, 2017). But as long as you're patient with yourself, the healthy habits you replace it with will soon become second nature.

If you have anxiety and depression, getting treatment for these will help you with your overthinking (Team Tony, n.d.). Remember the social anxiety solutions we talked about in Chapter 6 and see if the CBT and relaxation and self-talk strategies help keep your thoughts from spiraling out of control.

You can also manage your overthinking by distracting yourself with activities you enjoy, starting and ending your day with positive affirmations, grounding yourself in the present, and taking hold of your negative emotions before they spiral out of control. All of these things will help you calm your worry spirals and replace them with confident beliefs about yourself and your abilities.

Change the Channel

The worst thing you can do as an overthinker is to tell yourself not to think the way you do (Morin, 2016). This will only push you further down the worry spiral. Instead, distract yourself by doing things that you enjoy.

Keeping an active mind and body is essential for our overall health (Hurst, 2017). So, go for a jog or a bike ride. Swim laps at the pool. Solve a jigsaw puzzle. Listen to an audiobook. Learn a new language. Do something that makes you happy and releases your pent-up energy. By funneling your energy away from your worries, you'll help yourself feel at ease. This way, you'll be less likely to return to stressful thoughts, even after finishing your activity.

Use Daily Positive Affirmations

Repeating daily affirmations is one of the best methods to overcome overthinking (Hurst, 2017; McKibben, 2015;

Team Tony, n.d.). It encourages you to harness your inner power to change your negative thought patterns into positive ones.

To get started, stand in front of a mirror and look yourself in the eyes if it feels natural, smile. Anything to keep you focused and relaxed. Then, repeat a positive mantra that applies to whatever struggles you're facing. If you're feeling overwhelmed about your thoughts, try saying, "My thoughts do not control me. I control them." Or, if you're worried about being inactive, remind yourself, "I am a human being, not a human doing." Keep it short, but say whatever you need to make yourself feel better.

Repeat these affirmations several times a day before you go to bed at night, and as soon as you wake up in the morning. This way, you'll lull yourself into better sleep and energize yourself to face your challenges during the day. Soon, they'll be so ingrained in your mind that you won't just say these words. You'll believe them.

Live in the Moment

Overthinking often comes from rehashing the past or obsessing over the future (Team Tony, n.d.). But once you learn to live in the present, you'll cast these worries aside and shift your focus to the great things in your life that are happening right now. Take a look around you. Notice all of the things you have to be thankful for, like sunny weather, an adorable pet, a shelf full of books, or a comfy couch to lie on. The more you focus on these, the less likely you'll waste your time worrying about a past you can't change or a future you can't predict.

Whenever you're doing mundane activities, like getting dressed or walking to the bus, it's tempting to fill your mind with past and future worries. Hurst (2017) suggests grounding yourself in the present by narrating each thing that you do, taking note of every muscle movement. For example, if you're getting dressed and start to worry about what you'll order for dinner tonight, don't let yourself dwell on this. Create an internal monologue that describes each action of rolling up your pant leg, stretching your sock, pulling it onto your foot, hiking it as far as it will go up to your calf, then unrolling your pant leg and grabbing the next sock. Continue this narration until the anxious feeling passes.

Still, having trouble stopping the worry spiral? Practice mindful breathing-based activities like yoga, tai-chi, or guided meditation. (Clark & Lehmann, 2019; PsychAlive, 2015). Any type of breathing exercise you do will decrease your cortisol levels and increase your melatonin, helping you sleep. It'll also help you increase your self-awareness, improve your focus, and help you recognize your power to change your mind.

Control Your Emotions

Like I've said before, you can't control what happens to you out in the world. But you can manage your reactions to what happens to you.

Whenever you start experiencing a negative, unproductive emotion like anxiety, don't deny it and shove it to the back of your mind (Guerra, 2018; Morin, 2016; Team Tony, n.d.). Think about what makes you feel anxious and whether or not it's reasonable to react this way. Once you've figured out the why questions, you can start to ask the questions. What can you do to replace that negative thought with a positive one?

For example, if you're worried that your partner doesn't love you anymore, ask yourself why you think this. Have they done or said anything to prove this? Even if they have, think about some other reasons why they might be acting this way. For example, if they seem more distant, think about what else is going on in their life. Is their grandfather sick? Are they working on a stressful project at work? Are they working on a stressful project at home, like redesigning your kitchen or building a new deck? If nothing else comes to mind, talk to them about it to see if you can get to the root of the issue. Focus on listening to their side instead of rambling on how it makes you feel or accusing you of not paying enough attention.

Once you've found the root of the problem, replace the nagging thought in your mind with this realization. Each time you start to ask, "Why don't they love me anymore?"

correct yourself and say, "They love me. They're just worried about their grandpa." It's also helpful to remind yourself of all the ways they do love. For example, they may be acting more distant than usual, but they may still want to cuddle on the couch after work. Maybe they even ask you how your day was and take an interest in your latest project. Perhaps they still leave you goofy notes on the bathroom mirror or make you a cup of breakfast tea just the way you like it. If you look for the positive evidence, you'll find it. And this will help you overcome your worries.

Even if your partner doesn't want to talk about what's bothering them, give them the space to be with their thoughts, and don't blame yourself for their behavior. This can be difficult, especially if you've had a partner abandon you in the past. But give your new partner (and yourself) the benefit of the doubt. Remember that history won't always repeat itself. Go for a run, practice some diagrammatic breathing, or repeat your daily affirmations to take your mind off your relationship worries.

If you really feel the need to rehash negative emotions in your head, talk to a friend about your feelings instead. Voicing your fears out loud will take some weight off your chest and prevent you from spiraling out of control. You may even gain a new perspective on your problems in the process, where your friend points out options you hadn't considered before.

Studies show that you're less likely to worry throughout your day if you give yourself 20 minutes to get your worries out of your system (Clark & Lehmann, 2019). If you don't want to or can't talk to a friend or other trusted person, try writing your feelings down in a journal. Fret as much as you like. Then distract yourself the rest of the day with other things.

You might also find it helpful to write down all of the critical thoughts you have about yourself (PsychAlive, 2015). Frame them as second-person statements, so you see them from an outside perspective. For example, write, "You are weird and unlikable" instead of "I am weird and unlikable." Then, pretend you're giving advice to a friend who said this about themselves. What affirmation would you give them to help them feel better? For example, you might say, "I am a unique individual. I don't sacrifice my quirks to fit the status quo." Complete this exercise for all your negative thoughts about yourself. Do this every day until you see your supposed flaws in a more positive light.

Finally, it's important to remind yourself that worrying is not a means to an end (Guerra, 2018; Hakki, 2018). You can let go once events and conversations are no longer relevant to your life. Ask yourself if you can fix a mistake that's been made. If you can, brainstorm solutions, make a plan, then test it out and see if it works. If not, let it go, learn from it, and do better next time.

As you work to change your negative thought patterns, remember that nothing has meaning unless you give it meaning (McKibben, 2015). If you believe your negative thoughts and emotions, these will become your truth. If you believe your positive thoughts and feelings, these will become your truth. It's your choice which truth to take. But instead of agonizing over this choice, remind yourself of the peace of mind you'll receive when you decide to stop over-thinking and start facing your daily challenges with the confidence you need to be successful.

9

DEFENSE MECHANISMS

Overthinking isn't the only way we try to escape from our daily struggles. Even if we don't overwhelm our minds with negative thoughts, we can still protect ourselves from our reality by denying the consequences of our actions, burying our negative emotions, or disengaging from the world around us. These are all common types of defense mechanisms.

Defense mechanisms are cognitive processes that temporarily allow you to avoid dealing with trauma, stress, or anxieties (Grohol, 2019; Krauss Whitbourne, 2011; Team Tony, 2015). Sometimes you consciously try to protect yourself from these unacceptable thoughts and feelings. Other times, your brain does this automatically. You may never realize you're using a defense mechanism until someone points it out to you.

"We use defense mechanisms to protect ourselves from our traumatic or stressful realities (Du Preez, 2020)."

Some of the most common forms include:

Avoidance: this mechanism is nearly universal. It happens when you avoid an issue by procrastinating, changing the subject, or maintaining a false illusion of happiness.

Denial: another common mechanism, this occurs when you protect yourself from facing the facts by pretending they're not real. You then avoid situations where you might have to confront these facts. For example, you claim you're only a social smoker, but avoid going to the doctor who told you to quit.

Repression: this goes one step further than denial. You bury a negative experience in your subconscious to avoid the pain of remembering it, even if it gives you depression or anxiety. This is often the case with phobias. You might repress your near-drowning experience as a child, but spend your adult life being afraid of water.

Projection: this happens when you blame someone or something else for your insecurities. You do this by transferring these feelings onto them and being critical. For example, you criticize your teenage son for being lazy because you feel insecure about being unemployed. Or, you ask a stranger what they're staring at when you are self-conscious about a pimple on your face.

Displacement: you shift your emotions from the person or situation that's bothering you to someone or something that has nothing to do with it. This is especially common when you take out your frustrations from work by honking at the slow driver in front of you or kicking your recycling bin.

Reaction formation: you try to hide your shame by doing or saying the complete opposite of what you think. Maybe you pretend to despise a work colleague that you're secretly in love with. Or maybe you secretly despise the head of the PTA but still try to win their approval.

Rationalization: you make excuses to try and justify your bad behavior. For example, you shoplift from a store and claim that it's okay because the owners are already wealthy.

Intellectualization: this is similar to rationalization. But instead, you try to think away negative emotions, such as saying, "He was old anyway" after your grandfather dies.

Regression: instead of dealing with negative emotions, you revert to an early stage of development by acting like a child. This includes stomping out of the room during an argument or pulling your blankets over your head when you're scared.

Dissociation: when you're overwhelmed, you disengage from your body through depersonalization or your environment through derealization. This can include escaping into your daydreams to avoid confronting an abusive partner or a demanding career.

Compartmentalization: a milder form of dissociation, where you act like certain parts of yourself have a different set of values. For example, you might call yourself a socialist and vote for left-wing political parties. But you also buy designer clothes, which only exist because of capitalism.

Sublimation: you find socially acceptable outlets for your 'unacceptable' feelings, like joking about your fear of commitment or joining a boxing club to vent your anger issues.

Depending on the type and severity, defense mechanisms have their benefit (Team Tony, 2015). They stop you from doing or saying things you might regret. But they essentially put off the inevitable negative emotions you'll have to face someday. If left to their own devices, they can easily fuck up your life. That's why it's essential to identify where these coping mechanisms come from, so you can brainstorm better ways to manage your insecurities.

WHY WE HAVE THEM

Sigmund and Anna Freud were the first experts to identify defense mechanisms and suggest theories about where they come from (Krauss Whitbourne, 2011; Theodore, 2019). They argued that humans will do anything to gain pleasure and avoid pain. As a result, we turn to coping strategies to protect our ego, which is our sense of self.

Because they are found in people across ages and cultures, psychologists believe our defense mechanisms have a biological basis. This may also explain why so many of them happen unconsciously. Yet, while everyone has times where they act childishly during an argument, not everyone will consistently avoid conflict by throwing tantrums and slamming doors. Whether or not you let these defense mechanisms control your life depends on your level of emotional security.

Emotionally secure people are in control of their thoughts and feelings (Buddaeus, 2020). If they encounter a stressful situation, they may struggle temporarily, but they can easily bounce back from it. Emotionally insecure people, on the other hand, don't bounce back. Stressful situations scar their psyches, causing them to see the world as threatening and the people in it as cruel, selfish, and untrustworthy. As they shut the world out and turn inward, they tap into their negative emotional drives. They become aggressive, arrogant, neurotic, and self-centered. They can't deal with their world as it is. They can only cope with it by taking out their anger on others, intellectualizing their pessimism with philosophical theories, or composing sad piano songs.

We often develop these emotionally insecure behaviors as children (Branden, 1988). Let's say that your parents were abusive. To avoid the nightmare of your home life, you learned to "play dead," numbing yourself to your daily trauma through dissociation. Through no fault of your own, you become alienated from your true self. You hope that by doing so, this will save you from your painful emotions. But, without the proper psychological guidance, the suppression of your feelings can cause you to grow into an adult who distrusts the world. You may displace or project your fears onto others, taking out your aggression on them and/or accusing them of hating you. Whatever defense mechanisms you use, they are all misplaced safety measures to make you forget about or make up for your traumatic past.

When you grow up feeling emotionally insecure and lacking self-esteem, your defensive mechanisms aren't just triggered when you dwell on your inner thoughts (Buddaeus, 2020; Del Guercio, 2018; Team Tony, 2015). They are also more likely to appear whenever you face an external situation with uncertain outcomes or features that threaten your fundamental beliefs.

This is especially common in cognitive dissonance situations, where a different perspective challenges your worldview with more reliable evidence. This "external truth" cannot exist with your own truth. But instead of accepting the external truth, you cling even harder to your own truth, denying anyone or anything the chance to knock it off its pedestal.

"Cognitive dissonance makes you disengage from the world and look inward to find your source of truth (Smith, 2018)."

Let's say that, like every teenager, you struggled to find your place in the world. You needed a role model to hold yourself up to and found it in your favorite movie star. They seemed confident, well-spoken, and classy—just like you wanted to be. You modeled your fashion, speech, behavior, and interests after them, using them to inspire you on your path to adult success. Then, something terrible happens. Your idol is named in a sex scandal, is caught selling drugs, or maybe even injures someone in a DUI. Even when the evidence against them is pretty strong, you cannot bear the thought that the person you admired so much and tried so hard to be like could do something terrible. So, you resort to denying the evidence rather than your hero has fallen from their pedestal.

While they seem like good temporary fixes for long-term problems, defense mechanisms really are just temporary fixes (Buddaceus, 2020; Grohol, 2019). They don't do anything to help you move beyond your childhood trauma or accept that you need a new role model. They help you avoid threats, but they also prevent you from attaining rewards. And in severe cases, they can lead to mental health issues, such as multiple personality disorder, post-traumatic stress disorder, or any form of anxiety disorder.

That's why it's essential to identify these coping behaviors sooner rather than later. Once you know which ones you have and why you use them, you can gain a better hold on your thought processes and face your fears rather than run from them.

HOW WE CAN OVERCOME THEM

Defense mechanisms aren't the easiest insecurities to overcome, especially when you're used to unconsciously repressing bad memories or rationalizing petty theft. Plus, they can be associated with several deeper psychological issues. This is why it's essential to talk to a professional about your habits to figure out the best plan to address your specific needs.

Still, there are some tips to keep in mind that can help you gain a better hold on your defense mechanisms. This includes taking responsibility for your thought patterns, replacing your pathological mechanisms with more mature options, and learning to reduce your stress.

Own Your Thoughts and Actions

The first step toward managing your defense mechanisms is to take responsibility for your thoughts and actions (Team Tony, 2015). Don't blame other people or outside forces. Instead, do some soul searching to figure out why you feel and act the way you do.

This is particularly useful for defense mechanisms like displacement, projection, rationalization, and intellectualization. It's a lot easier to shift your insecurities onto an easy target, like accusing your partner of making fun of your bad haircut or blaming old age on your grandfather's death. But you might feel better about your hairstyle if you remind yourself that you're the only one who's ever said anything negative about it. You'll realize that it's normal and healthy to grieve the loss of a loved one, no matter how old they are.

You may not feel any better about either situation. But by getting used to facing your problems, you'll gain the emotional security you need to deal with them in a healthy way. This way, you'll learn to bounce back after your mourning period or your few days of obsessive hat-wearing. You won't be permanently weighed down by unhelpful coping mechanisms.

Identify Mature Mechanisms

Not all defense mechanisms are created equal. Some are useful; others aren't. Some are useful only in moderation.

For example, sublimation helps you channel your fears into something productive, like focusing your anger through boxing (Team Tony, 2015). This way, you can feel better about your emotions and achieve new goals in the process. But when used in excess, sublimation can keep you from confronting major problems or taking direct action to solve them. You may be so busy working on your jabs and upper-cuts that you never sort out where your anger comes from and whether you can address your anger issues. And the longer you keep it bottled up, the more likely it will explode out of you at an unknown time––even outside the boxing ring.

To separate the useful defense mechanisms from the less useful ones, psychiatrist George Eman Vaillant proposed four classifications: pathological (or highly abnormal), immature, neurotic, or mature (cited in Buddaeus, 2020). Pathological defense mechanisms (ex: denial) are the most dangerous because they severely distort reality. Immature defense mechanisms (ex: projection) can cause antisocial behaviors like bullying or passive-aggressiveness, but don't affect your perception as severely as the pathological ones. Similarly, neurotic defense mechanisms (ex: rationalization) can distort your perception through obsessive behavior, but in a milder form.

It's mature defense mechanisms that are the most rational and beneficial. These include behaviors like self-deprecating humor, which allows you to talk about uncomfortable subjects comfortably, and altruism, which makes you feel better about yourself by making others feel good. Like sublimation, they have their flaws when used in excess. But they provide less severe complications than the other types of defense mechanisms.

So next time you hear about your favorite movie star's latest drug troubles, don't deny them. Make a tasteful joke of the situation by turning it back to your irrational obsession. It doesn't even have to be a good joke. For example, you might say, "Well, [so-so] used to be my hero, but they had to trade my love for the heroine." By using a bad pun, you're not condoning what the actor did. Still, you're allowing yourself to express your disappointment in a way that might make you feel better about the situation.

And if you can't find humor in the situation? Make yourself feel better by volunteering with a community organization that helps recovering addicts or make a donation to your local rehab center. Use your disappointment in your hero as an excuse to help people who are suffering from similar actions.

By replacing your pathological, immature, and neurotic mechanisms with mature mechanisms, you'll be able to ease yourself into facing negative situations without stressing yourself out. You'll learn to laugh at yourself and find joy in spreading positivity. Plus, you'll find a more productive outlet for your worries, bringing you the peace of mind you deserve.

Manage Your Stress

Many defense mechanisms, like regression, are a product of stress (Krauss Whitbourne, 2011). The relaxation techniques from Chapter 6 and self-care suggestions from Chapter 3 are great ways to help you clear your mind. With a calm, positive mindset, you'll find it much easier to confront your negative thoughts. Or at least substitute harmful coping methods with more positive ones.

Defense mechanisms don't disappear overnight. They may never go away completely. But once you find the path that works for you, you can quit relying on temporary fixes and find real solutions to overcome your insecurities.

CONCLUSION

Insecurities are a true pain in the ass. They fill you with fears, doubts, and worries about your qualities and abilities. They trick you into thinking that you're unworthy of love, that you don't deserve success, that social interactions will literally kill you, or that it's okay to steal––as long as you take from the rich. But they don't have to trap you forever.

No matter what your insecurities are, you can overcome them by first identifying their root causes. Maybe you inherited them from your parents. Maybe you learned them to help you cope with bullying. Or perhaps you picked up bad habits from trying to be a social media influencer. Whatever it is, use this knowledge to create your personal solution. Try out a few different options, then choose the one that makes the most sense for your needs.

You may not get it right the first time. Or the second. Or the tenth. Or the three-hundredth. But don't give up. Remind yourself that you are in control of your mindset. Positive thoughts create positive beliefs, which inspire positive actions, which breed positive habits. So, take a deep breath, repeat your positive affirmations, and ground yourself at the moment. Then try again. Who knows? The three-hundred-and-first time just might be the one that helps you find the confidence you've always looked for.

Like Brown (2007) argues, self-confidence is born from courage. These days, we tend to think of courage as a one-off heroic deed, like slaying a dragon or tackling a purse thief outside the mall. But real courage is more about inner strength. It's about speaking your mind by speaking from the heart.

And when your heart tells you to say "fuck you" to your insecurities? Embrace all the wacky and wonderful things that make you? Believe that you can create a happy, self-assured life for yourself? Listen to it. This is the gateway to greatness.

I hope you've enjoyed reading this book. Please consider leaving a review on Amazon if you found it helpful. I'd love to hear from you.

Until next time, keep on living your best life. Trust me: you deserve it.

REFERENCES

AIPC. (2019, November 14). The psychology of bragging. *Counselling Connection.* https://www.counsellingconnection.com/index.php/2019/11/14/the-psychology-of-bragging/

Altmann, G. (2017). Woman face insight compared to. In *Pixabay.* https://pixabay.com/photos/woman-face-insight-compared-to-2944070/

Bacon, L. (2014, October 6). The comparison trap: How to enjoy (and not envy) the success of others. *Adobe 99U.* https://99u.adobe.com/articles/33341/comparison-trap-envy-jealous-success-coworkers-friends

Barucija, E. (2019, September 16). Why insecure people brag so much? *Gildshire Magazines.* https://www.gildshire.com/why-insecure-people-brag-so-much/

Becker-Phelps, L. (2016). *Insecure in love: how anxious attachment can make you feel jealous, needy, and worried and what you can do about it.* New Harbinger Publications. https://www.pdfdrive.com/insecure-in-love-how-anxious-attachment-can-make-you-feel-jealous-needy-and-worried-and-what-you-can-do-about-it-d175944742.html

Beliaikin, A. (2018, August 13). Free person. In *Unsplash.* https://unsplash.com/photos/ze_IO-_tcjw

Branden, N. (1988). *How to raise your self-esteem: The proven, action-orientated approach to greater self-respect and self-confidence.* Bantam. https://www.pdfdrive.com/how-to-raise-your-self-esteem-the-proven-action-oriented-approach-to-greater-self-respect-and-self-confidence-e194529021.html

Bridges to Recovery. (2018). Causes of social anxiety. *Bridges to Recovery.* https://www.bridgestorecovery.com/social-anxiety/causes-social-anxiety/

Brown, B. (2007). *I thought it was just me (but it isn't): Women reclaiming power and courage in a culture of shame.* Gotham Books. https://www.pdfdrive.com/i-thought-it-was-just-me-women-reclaiming-power-and-courage-in-a-culture-of-shame-e184522836.html

Brown, B. (2010). *The gifts of imperfection: Let go of who you think you're supposed to be and embrace who you are.* Hazelden. https://www.pdfdrive.com/the-gifts-of-imperfection-let-go-of-who-you-think-youre-supposed-to-be-and-embrace-who-you-are-e158952942.html

Buckley, C. (2018, July 31). 13 approval seeking behaviours you need to stop. *Live Your True Story.* https://www.liveyourtruestory.com/13-approval-seeking-behaviours-you-need-to-stop-confidence/

Buddaeus, K. (2020, May 11). Emotional insecurity, defense mechanisms and disorders. *Medium.* https://medium.com/illumination/emotional-insecurity-defense-mechanisms-and-disorders-75c77aead8ed

Buscher, N. (2018). Woman reaching hand above water during daytime photo. In *Unsplash.* https://unsplash.com/photos/AUM5vcnuYd4

Camara Wilkins, M. (2017, July 3). What it means to be enough. *Melissa Camara Wilkins.* https://melissacamarawilkins.com/what-it-means-to-be-enough/

Chen, Y. (2018, April 16). Undo the lie of not being good enough. *Medium.* https://medium.com/swlh/undo-the-lie-of-not-being-good-enough-837d85401f96

Clark, K., & Lehmann, C. (2019, October 10). The psychology behind chronic overthinking (and how to stop it). *Mydomaine.* https://www.mydomaine.com/overthinking-hacks

Collinson, D. L. (2003). Identities and insecurities: Selves at work. *Organization, 10*(3), 527–547. ResearchGate. https://doi.org/https://doi.org/10.1177/13505084030103010

Cuncic, A. (2019a, September 30). *4 tips for practicing diaphragmatic breathing for social anxiety.* Verywell Mind. https://www.verywellmind.com/how-do-i-practice-deep-breathing-for-anxiety-3024389

Cuncic, A. (2019b, November 26). *Chill out: How to use progressive muscle relaxation to quell anxiety.* Verywell Mind. https://www.verywellmind.com/how-do-i-practice-progressive-muscle-relaxation-3024400

Cuncic, A. (2020a, March 18). Simple steps to start practicing guided imagery for anxiety relief. Verywell Mind. https://www.verywellmind.com/how-do-you-practice-guided-imagery-for-anxiety-3024396

Cuncic, A. (2020b, May 30). *Situations that can trigger social anxiety.* Verywell Mind. https://www.verywellmind.com/which-situations-trigger-anxiety-3024887

Davret, B. (2019, December 4). How to get over the fear of not being good enough. *Medium.* https://medium.com/writtenpersuasion/how-to-get-over-the-fear-of-not-being-good-enough-615826d85363

Del Guercio, G. (2018, April 22). Do you use any of these 7 defense mechanisms? *Aleteia.* https://aleteia.org/2018/04/22/7-common-defense-mechanisms-that-cause-anxiety/

Douglas, N. (2019, November 28). Overcome imposter syndrome with a "brag file." *Lifehacker Australia.* https://www.lifehacker.com.au/2019/11/overcome-imposter-syndrome-with-a-brag-file/

Du Preez, P. (2020). Person in brown long sleeve shirt covering face with hand. In *Unsplash.* https://unsplash.com/photos/NQTphr4Pr60

Erfurt, C. (2018). Man covering face with both hands while sitting on bench. In *Unsplash.* https://unsplash.com/photos/sxQz2VfoFBE

Espinosa, I. (2017). A person drowns underwater. In *Unsplash.* https://unsplash.com/photos/rX12B5uX7QM

Felman, A. (2018, February 5). Social anxiety disorder: Causes, symptoms, and treatment. *MedicalNewsToday.* https://www.medicalnewstoday.com/articles/176891#overcoming-anxiety

Fernando. (2018). Man beside white frame window. In *Unsplash.* https://unsplash.com/photos/6x2iKGi6SPU

Geddis, K. (2018, August 20). The REAL reason we look for validation and approval...and how to overcome it. *Karen Geddis.* http://karengeddis.com/why-we-look-for-validation

Ghose, T. (2015, May 15). Braggers gonna brag, but it usually backfires. *LiveScience.* https://www.livescience.com/50848-bragging-annoys-people.html

Grohol, J. M. (2018, October 8). 15 common defense mechanisms. *PsychCentral*. https://psychcentral.com/lib/15-common-defense-mechanisms/

Guay, M. (2018, August 29). 10 ways to stop thinking you're not "good enough." *PsychCentral*. https://psychcentral.com/blog/10-ways-to-stop-thinking-youre-not-good-enough/

Guerra, J. (2018, February 21). Experts say these 5 things mean you're overthinking to the point of exhaustion. *Elite Daily*. https://www.elitedaily.com/p/5-signs-you-over-think-to-the-point-of-exhausting-yourself-according-to-experts-8278012

Hain, J. (2015a). Cloud insecurity negativity. In *Pixabay*. https://pixabay.com/illustrations/cloud-insecurity-negativity-fears-705728/

Hain, J. (2015b). Shame child small. In *Pixabay*. https://pixabay.com/illustrations/shame-child-small-criticism-799099/

Hakki, M. (2018, August 8). 10 obvious signs of overthinking and how to deal with it. *IHeartIntelligence.Com*. https://iheartintelligence.com/signs-of-overthinking/

Ho, J. (2019, November 2). Why we self-sabotage. *Psychology Today*. https://www.psychologytoday.com/ca/blog/unlock-your-true-motivation/201911/why-we-self-sabotage

Hopper, S. (2019, June 26). What happens when we stop seeking validation on social media. *Medium*. https://medium.com/@thestevenpost/what-happens-when-we-stop-seeking-validation-on-social-media-1a74e6c605ca

Hurst, K. (2017, September 19). *How to stop overthinking and overcome anxiety now*. The Law Of Attraction.Com; GreaterMinds. https://www.thelawofattraction.com/stop-overthinking-overcome-anxiety/

Iwata, B. A. (1987). Negative reinforcement in applied behavior analysis: An emerging technology. *Journal of Applied Behavior Analysis, 20*(4), 361–378. https://doi.org/10.1901/jaba.1987.20-361

Jacob, C. (2019, January 4). *Why are people insecure? 7 root causes of insecurity*. UpJourney. https://upjourney.com/why-are-people-insecure

Jeschke, C. (2018). Man standing on gray rock looking at mountain peak. In *Unsplash*. https://unsplash.com/photos/32mdWsp3Ogw

Kabat-Zinn, J. (2013). *Full catastrophe living* (2nd ed.). Bantam Books. https://www.pdfdrive.com/full-catastrophe-living-d168188903.html

Kelly, M. (2004). *The rhythm of life: Living every day with passion and purpose*. Simon & Schuster. https://www.pdfdrive.com/the-rhythm-of-life-living-every-day-with-passion-and-purpose-e162803026.html

Krauss Whitbourne, S. (2011, October 22). The essential guide to defense mechanisms. *Psychology Today.* https://www.psychologytoday.com/ca/blog/fulfillment-any-age/201110/the-essential-guide-defense-mechanisms

Krauss Whitbourne, S. (2012, July 28). Bragging, when is it OK and when is it not OK? *Psychology Today.* https://www.psychologytoday.com/ca/blog/fulfillment-any-age/201207/bragging-when-is-it-ok-and-when-is-it-not-ok

Krauss Whitbourne, S. (2015, November 17). 4 signs that someone is probably insecure. *Psychology Today.* https://www.psychologytoday.com/ca/blog/fulfillment-any-age/201511/4-signs-someone-is-probably-insecure

Krauss Whitbourne, S. (2018, March 31). Why people hate humblebragging. *Psychology Today.* https://www.psychologytoday.com/us/blog/fulfillment-any-age/201803/why-people-hate-humblebragging

Kwak, J. (2014, October 16). How to promote yourself without bragging. *GovLoop.* https://www.govloop.com/promote-without-bragging/

Laderer, A. (2018, February 20). 4 signs you're self-sabotaging (+ how to stop). *Talkspace.* https://www.talkspace.com/blog/4-signs-youre-self-sabotaging-how-to-stop/

Lamia, M. C. (2013, July 13). Jealousy and envy: The emotions of comparison and contrast. *Psychology Today.* https://www.psychologytoday.com/ca/blog/intense-emotions-and-strong-feelings/201307/jealousy-and-envy-the-emotions-comparison-and

LaRue, B. (2017). A woman holding a heart. In *Unsplash*. https://unsplash.com/photos/jMd3WS9LBcc

Lauton, E. (2016). Woman holding brown umbrella. In *Unsplash*. https://unsplash.com/photos/TyQ-0lPp6e4

Le Duc, Chinh. (2016). Boy leaning on white chair. In *Unsplash*. https://unsplash.com/photos/TV1QYUtTxJ8

Leahy, R. L. (2014, October 20). How to overcome your social anxiety. Psychology Today. https://www.psychology-today.com/ca/blog/anxiety-files/201410/how-overcome-your-social-anxiety

LinkedIn Sales Navigator. (2017). Two men talking. In *Unsplash*. https://unsplash.com/photos/W3Jl3jREpDY

Mayo Clinic. (2017). *Social anxiety disorder (social phobia) - Symptoms and causes.* Mayo Clinic. https://www.may-oclinic.org/diseases-conditions/social-anxiety-disorder/symptoms-causes/syc-20353561

McCutcheon, S. (2018). Person holding fan of U.S. dollars banknote. In *Unsplash*. https://unsplash.com/photos/rItGZ4vquWk

McKibben, S. (2015, July 3). 15 signs you're an over-thinker even if you don't feel you are. *Lifehack*. https://www.life-hack.org/287116/15-signs-youre-over-thinker-even-you-dont-feel-you-are

Morin, A. (2016, February 12). 6 tips to stop overthinking. *Psychology Today.* https://www.psychologytoday.com/ca/blog/what-mentally-strong-people-dont-do/201602/6-tips-stop-overthinking

Mozhvilo, E. (2020). Gold and silver round frame magnifying glass. In *Unsplash.* https://unsplash.com/photos/j06g-LuKK0GM

Nair, R. (2013, March 28). Why do we seek validation and approval? *RagsNair.* https://ragsnair.com/2013/03/28/validation/

Penguiny, L. (n.d.). The best article ever written about bragging. *Less Penguiny.* Retrieved June 23, 2020, from https://www.lesspenguiny.com/articles/best-article-on-bragging

Plata, M. (2018, July 11). The psychology of humblebragging. *Psychology Today.* https://www.psychologytoday.com/us/blog/the-gen-y-psy/201807/the-psychology-humblebragging

PsychAlive. (2015, July 7). Are you overthinking everything? *PsychAlive.* https://www.psychalive.org/are-you-over-thinking-everything/

Rauch, J. (2017, January 24). What causes social anxiety? *Talkspace.* https://www.talkspace.com/blog/what-causes-social-anxiety/

Raypole, C. (2019, November 21). Self-sabotage: 17 things to know. *Healthline.* https://www.healthline.com/health/self-sabotage#takeaway

Ries, J. (2019, November 21). Here's what happens to your body when you overthink. HuffPost Canada. https://www.huffingtonpost.ca/entry/overthinking-effects_l_5dd2bd67e4b0d2e79f90fe1b

Rudolph, K. (2018, July 3). 5 reasons why it feels so darn hard to love yourself sometimes. *YourTango.* https://www.yourtango.com/experts/kellyrudolph/5-reasons-hard-to-love-yourself-and-how-to-make-self-love-easier

Schuster, S. (2018, August 22). 17 things people don't realize you're doing because you're overthinking. *The Mighty.* https://themighty.com/2018/08/signs-of-anxiety-over-thinking/

Smith, T. (2018). Woman wearing black and multicolored blouse and blue denim jeans facing mirror inside white concrete room. In *Unsplash.* https://unsplash.com/photos/C44h1ZmlFF0

Smith, M., Segal, J., & Shubin, J. (2019, November). Social Anxiety Disorder. *HelpGuide.* https://www.helpguide.org/articles/anxiety/social-anxiety-disorder.htm

Socha, A. (2016). Cup podium trophy. In *Pixabay.* https://pixabay.com/illustrations/cup-podium-trophy-gold-

golden-1615074/

Staddon, J. E. R., & Cerutti, D. T. (2003). Operant conditioning. *Annual Review of Psychology, 54*(1), 115–144. https://doi.org/10.1146/annurev.psych.54.101601.145124

Steph Social. (2020, March 7). Do you self sabotage? Signs of self sabotaging behaviour. *Steph Social*. https://stephsocial.com/2020/03/07/self-sabotage/

Strauss Cohen, I. (2018, July 13). How to let go of the need for approval. *Psychology Today*. https://www.psychologytoday.com/ca/blog/your-emotional-meter/201807/how-let-go-the-need-approval

Suval, L. (2012, September 20). What drives our need for approval? *PsychCentral*. https://psychcentral.com/blog/what-drives-our-need-for-approval/

Swan, T. (n.d.). Jealousy and envy. *Teal Swan*. https://teal-swan.com/resources/articles/jealousy-and-envy/

Team Tony. (2015, December 23). 10 surprising defense mechanisms & how to identify them. *Tony Robbins*. https://www.tonyrobbins.com/mind-meaning/10-common-defense-mechanisms/#:~:text=Many%2520people%2520include%2520projection%2520in

Team Tony. (n.d.) 7 strategies to stop overthinking everything. *Tony Robbins*. Retrieved June 24, 2020, from https://www.tonyrobbins.com/mental-health/how-to-stop-overthinking/